PINK HIGHWAYS

Also by Michael Lane

Mad Monks on the Road (with Jim Crotty)
Monk (magazine, with Jim Crotty)

PINK HIGHWAYS

Tales of Queer Madness
On the Open Road

MICHAEL LANE

A Birch Lane Press Book
Published by Carol Publishing Group

DISCLAIMER

The persons and events in this book are factual. In a few cases I have changed a name or location to avoid unwanted exposure.

Copyright © 1995 by Michael Lane

A Birch Lane Press Book
Published by Carol Publishing Group
Birch Lane Press is a registered trademark of Carol Communications, Inc.
Editorial Offices: 600 Madison Avenue, New York, N.Y. 10022
Sales & Distribution Offices: 120 Enterprise Avenue, Secaucus, N.J. 07094
In Canada: Canadian Manda Group, One Atlantic Avenue, Suite 105, Toronto, Ontario M6K 3E7
Queries regarding rights and permissions should be addressed to Carol Publishing Group, 600 Madison Avenue, New York, N.Y. 10022

Carol Publishing Group books are available at special discounts for bulk purchases, sales promotions, fund-raising, or educational purposes. Special editions can be created to specifications. For details contact: Special Sales Department, Carol Publishing Group, 120 Enterprise Avenue, Secaucus, N.J. 07094

Manufactured in the United States of America
10 9 8 7 6 5 4 3 2 1

Library of Congress Cataloging-in-Publication Data

Lane, Michael, 1950–
    Pink highways : tales of queer madness on the open road / by Michael Lane.
        p   cm.
    "A Birch Lane Press book."
    ISBN 1–55972–263–0
    1. Lane, Michael, 1950–   —Journeys.   2. Voyages and travels.
3. Gays—Travel.   I. Title.
G465.L35   1995
910.4—dc20   94–20516
                                            CIP

DEDICATION

To Viktor Fidele

CONTENTS

Contents

PART ONE

1

Burn, Baby, Burn

Life made a mistake. I was supposed to have a ten-inch dick, muscles made of iron, a full head of hair and no wrinkles and lines, ever. Not even now, while I'm sitting on the side of the road with a small crack in my rib under the blazing sun waiting for that dirty dog of a Greyhound to come and rescue me from this town.

I shouldn't feel like this. The ticket man was passing cute, the three riders in line aren't carrying guns or muttering to themselves, and the one lone, card-carrying lunatic digging through the Dumpster for cans didn't hit me up for change. It might even be a decent ride, but I feel like my back has hit the ground one too many times. Either that or I've had one too many fifty-nine-cent Taco Bell burritos go down the wrong way.

I can still see the stretch of barbed wire lying across the road a country block away and a small brushfire raging across the hill, licking a barn door where an old woman is soaking feed bags to keep them from catching fire. She's got two wannabe cowboys in faded jeans and sloppy black Stetsons dousing the barn with buckets of water. I almost hope the firemen don't come, but they will and I'll be glad I'm out of Grants Pass, Oregon, because someone's going to want my ass even more once the fire's out.

All of this because I gave a certain cowboy the eye.

Not just any eye. But the sort of deep-set liquid sapphire eyes embedded in a cave of longing that I sometimes flash at gnarly cowboys in the heat of a day.

I am trying to get through this nowhere of a small town. I want to get to San Francisco by Saturday; today's Friday and here I am in the wild West. But that's not the whole truth. I really have to get to New York by next Thursday to meet the Queen of Tantra herself, Annie Sprinkle, and drive to the march on Washington by the weekend. That's if I ever make it out of here alive.

So I thought I was doing good, cruising seventy miles an hour in my drive-away car, south on Interstate 5. I left behind my good friend and partner, Jim "the Mad Monk," with our three-ton motor home parked in Portland and made it all the way from there to Grants Pass in four easy hours late last night. Jim and I have been traveling for nine years in our tiny box of a home, living on the open road publishing Monk, the world's only mobile magazine.

It's time for a break, wouldn't you say, so I'm off on a solo spin for a week or two.

I stopped once for six Taco Bell bean-and-cheese burritos in Eugene and then once again for a hitchhiking longhair who I thought might be a faerie but wasn't. I slept in the car about a mile out of town, curled up in the backseat with my toes out the window while listening to the coyotes howl at the dust clouds and the passing semis stall on the pass.

By late morning I was raring to go, with more steam in me than a calliope, but the battery was dead. Even when a sweet young Mormon stopped and offered a jump the thing still wouldn't start because the starter was gone, too. So I was out of a car. Since it wasn't mine I felt like walking. So I did. I walked the few miles into town with my bag of clothes, reported the car to the drive-away car people and went into a former A&W Root Beer, only now it was just a cheap burger joint with really strong coffee—too strong for me.

A few cowboys were sitting in there, hunkered over their ashtrays, and no one looked any meaner than me, so I felt safe to go in. But when I went in I could feel all of the eyes on me, not in a welcoming sort of way, but a way that spelled trouble and lots of it. They didn't know how much I love trouble, so I helped myself to the gum machine and asked the waitress if they had any bottled spring water because I was tired of getting the runs every time I started in with new water in a new town with new germs.

The waitress was just some dumpy old broad—no beehive hairdo, no classic cat-eyed glasses, not even a chain-smoking broad—just a plain one in an ugly gray dress and a crucifix hanging off her neck. But she did have painted fingernails the color of a strawberry daiquiri and the tips of her eyelids had one of those mint-green shades of K-mart eye shadow on them.

"You're stunning," I said in a half whisper just to contradict my thoughts.

"If you want some bottled water go back to California. Ours is pure from the tap," she snapped.

Ouch. I liked her already. She might have been plain but she knew how to level a spring-water bottle drinker in one easy blow, and I wasn't even from California. I could tell that beneath her cool Christian demeanor was a nail-scratching bitch looking for a pair of balls to claw.

I just smiled, told her I would have a seat at the counter and was on my way to use the bathroom to wash the night off my face when two hefty porkers, fresh from downing ham-and-cheese omelets, came wobbling over from their counter stools. One, quite a bit older than the other, was picking between his teeth and had a nice-sized scar on the side of his forehead. They both looked like they had a midmorning beer buzz, mellow like hay. I could tell they'd been at the counter a bit too long from their bow-legged walks.

The younger one had a handsome face. Before I could stop myself I was giving him the eye a moment too long. The curve of his chin sported a day of whiskers and his lips were in a half-parted pout that looked so bedroom-perfect I was almost willing to look past my distaste for lard-eating, potbellied ranchers in order to take a peek down his pants. That's when it began. He caught my wanting look and I could feel their meanness long before they'd shoved me down to the floor.

Those two-fisted, belt-popping, white-assed cowboys walked side by side, headed straight for me and shouldered me hard enough to make me lose my balance. As if hitting the floor wasn't enough, one of them jammed his pointed boot into my weakest rib. All I remember was staring at their crotches, wondering how in God's name cowboys with no sense of style could have the most Goddamn tight-fitting jeans, biggest bulging baskets and perfectly round asses that'd be the envy of every size queen east of Memphis. They stood long enough for me to get an eyeful, their big old jelly bellies bouncing in my face.

I must have seemed like I was licking my wound, because the younger one said to me in a country, warm-as-butter drawl, "Sorry 'bout the accident!" Then they chuckled on out the door.

An accident it did not seem. No one even stared up from their coffee and I just lay on the floor, slightly bruised. I felt like lying there for a while. It offered a totally new perspective of the burger joint. I began noticing how much grease had built up on the underside of the grill and could see under the counter, watching people do the stuff they do while they're eating. People were thumping their fingers, twitching their hands, scratching their butts, kicking the counter with their feet, pulling bones or things that didn't taste right from their mouths and flinging them under the seats. I spotted all the holes in their boots and the smears of dog shit on their soles and I propped my head on my hand to take it easy and master the moment.

Five minutes passed and my pain was subsiding. I was loving the floor and the vast blight of unattended dirt that spread across the linoleum. A small column of ants made their way around the corner near the cash register and headed for the grill.

The waitress finally said, "Get up or get out." Not "You hurt?" or "You Okay?" Just "Get up." And not a tinge of sarcasm. She just let the words die there in a prudent way.

I complied with both requests, since the "accident" had taken away my appetite. Outside I began walking down the street for the Greyhound bus station, the outpatient ward of the universe, and I was enjoying the haze of a dust cloud that climbed toward the sun over the rolling landscape. The two porkers who shouldered me were suddenly driving alongside, not in a pickup or four-by-four or even in an old beat-up black Caddie, but in an un-American-as-you-can-get old Honda Civic with rusted doors. No gun rack, no antlers on the hood and no dusty medallion hanging from the rearview mirror. That's when I knew they were losers with no class at all.

"What the hell do you want?" I finally yelled a bit louder than I had planned.

"We thought you looked like you might need a ride," yelled the youngest while smacking on a piece of stale gum.

I stopped at a corner and stared down at the little rib-crunching shit and his ten-gallon hat. There was no way in hell I was about to get in that car with them. My face was beginning to flush shades of suicide red. I contemplated whether I had enough adrenaline to kick a hole through the door and plant my sneaker up his ass, where it belonged. But then I saw a sheriff cruising slowly down the street and reconsidered.

They saw him too. They looked a little sweaty. Maybe one too many unpaid tickets were crumpled under their dashboard.

"I think not! Besides, this little bitty ol' rusted Honda of yours looks like it's carrying all the cargo it can handle," I said as I crossed the street, confident that the sheriff would keep them out of my hair.

They pulled out and rolled on by, but not before giving me a middle-finger salute from the window.

I kept on walking and passed a gun shop with more bumper stickers, T-shirts and propaganda than guns. Up in the window was a T-shirt of Hitler with a caption saying EVERYBODY FOR GUN CONTROL RAISE YOUR RIGHT HAND, and a sign on the door read IF YOU VOTED FOR CLINTON DO NOT BOTHER SHOPPING HERE. I didn't plan on going in, but silently questioned just how in the hell they could tell who I voted for.

A few doors down was a Christian bookstore. Farther up the street were two old guys in full army camouflage and National Rifle Association armbands getting out of a Cherokee. They were flaunting their cause heavier than a whore under a street lamp and I wondered if they were selling rifles from the back of their Jeep. If they were, I was definitely in the mood for a big purchase.

I began to notice the number of stores with brass eagles, American flags or Bibles in the window. I began to count the number of cars with the little fish insignia on the back. And then I spotted a posted street sign that said NO SKATEBOARDS, NO BICYCLES and underneath, in aerosol black, sprayed in bold block lettering, NO FAGS.

Oops! That's when the panic rose. This was a gun-toting, flag-waving, Jesus-loving, fag-hating sort of town.

I was feeling conspicuous in my crotch-to-the-knee, baggy homeboy salmon-colored jeans, black turtleneck and freshly shaven head. I checked myself out in the reflection of a window and began an impromptu evaluation of whether I was passing straight, or if not, what was I?

I found myself wanting to appear like a tough mother with a possible mental disorder and a mean enough disposition to chew heads off rattlesnakes.

Passing one more gun shop with a motley crew of hunters who were loading up a pickup with camping gear and rifles, I abandoned my macho posturing with a gulp and scampered across the street. I headed north of town, lugging my thirty-five-pound shoulder bag and whistling a prayer to their Jesus.

Then the guys in the Honda reappeared at my tail, looking meaner than ever. They kept a menacing fifty feet behind while I trudged through town, keeping pace until I got on a long stretch of desolate road going out to the station. One of them took a string of firecrackers out of a sack as they pulled closer and hollered, "Dance!"

Now, I've been to a dance before where all of the girls lined up on one side of the room, then all of the other girls lined up on the other side of the room and then the music began. The girls all picked their partner and the whole room went on fire with girls dancing with girls.

It wasn't a dyke dance, either.

It was my junior high in Memphis and no boys would dance because it was too soon for boys to be dancing. You know, that age between bragging about pubic hair and actually having pubic hair. The boys had better things to do. They'd throw a string of lit firecrackers onto the gym floor in the middle of the dance. That's when things would really get wild, with those ponytailed pups tapping the hardwood floor over the ricocheting poppers. They'd go out into the hall in a big rush, trotting past the fireworks, screaming, their knees higher then their chins, their skirts rushing and the cruel boys cracking smiles while running from the Boys' Vice Principal.

Well, that's how I was dancing down to the bus station. They were popping Red Devils at my feet. I was swearing, throwing rocks and trotting high from every round of pops. They were cracking grins. The cute one, the one I'd made eyes at, was pulling stringers out of a sack deeper than God until they nearly drove over a strand of barbed-wire fence that was lying across the road about a block from the bus station. I knew those pokes were so lazy they couldn't be bothered with pulling the wire off the tarmac. Instead, they turned up a dirt road as I hurled one last stone at their rear, and damn if I didn't make a dent. They parked the Honda by a house on a slight hill opposite the station. I think one of them lived there.

I was not one bit happier to be rid of them. I didn't like dancing to crackers and I could smell the fire in my soul wanting to string those two porkers up by their blubbery toes and let the fat all drain to their heads until their eyes popped out. I was feeling more hate for those slime holes, more than I ever hated my stepdad for all of the poundings he gave me. I was walking fast for the station, not paying a bit of mind to the babble coming loose from my lips or the glazed look of defiance I held on my wrinkled face.

That's when I heard another string of pops.

Pained as I was, I turned my head and saw they'd let loose another package of firecrackers across the street. One of them was kicking his heels on the side of a bale of hay with a straw in his mouth. It was so Marlboro Country I was red with fury and I wanted my revenge.

The older one was getting down off his stump of hay. Without a word he wove a dusty trail toward a small barn, pulling at his low-riding jeans, so low I could see his cowboy cleavage peeking out. He was poking around the door, pulling out a handful of launchers that he braced up against the hay, aimed at me.

I didn't feel like watching another show of testosterone-fueled projectiles. I was walking again for the Greyhound, thinking about young girls dancing with firecrackers and mean-talking cheap shots in small towns in Oregon, when he lit the fuse. The whole damn thing exploded in the hay. I saw smoke coming up. A small fire

started licking the hay and spreading across dry brush.
An old woman leaned out from the house and started a
good-sized screaming fit. She beat at the flames while the
men tossed water on the barn by the bucketfuls.

"Burn, baby, burn," I chanted at the top of my lungs.
"I hope your porker balls roast in hell, you swine."

Oh, they were mad.

I close my eyes here at the station, waiting outside on
the island of concrete between the building and the bus
lane, smelling the sweet sanitized Pine-Sol from the toilets
inside. I touch a tender rib and listen for the diesel roar of
an oncoming bus. I wonder what got them going more,
the fear I was a spring-water-drinking Californian or the
fear I was a born-in-the-saddle, glad-to-be alive, flag-
waving, life-affirming queer.

2

Back of the Bus

One hour late, the bus arrives. It's full of afternoon sleepers who look like contortionists wrestling for a
bit of shut-eye in whatever way they can. A lot of single
eyes open and flash that expectant dread of whether I or
the three other new riders will interrupt their slumber by
sitting next to them. I have no choice, since every window
seat is taken. Someone's going to lose out.

It's my call and I like that. I peruse my unwilling
seatmates. No one is making inviting overtures. We've got
a weathered-looking lady in a macramé vest and house
slippers up at the front who undoubtedly has provided the
driver with hours of dreaded conversation, a woman and
her snotty-faced kid who definitely look like they're on the
lam, a good-looking single white male who seems possibly
psycho, a battery of Hispanic farm laborers each with
their heads cocked against the window in drooling slumber, and a dozen other travelers who look like your
average monster-truck-rally white-trash grandstanders.

I, two older ladies with blue hair and a Native
American who is going the distance to start a new life in

L.A. slowly make our way down the aisle. At the back of the bus I spot a lone gent spread across the coveted three seats. He must think that because he's at the back of the bus and next to the smelly toilet he'll be safe from intrusion.

He also happens to be the meanest-looking person on the bus.

I consider being near the toilet an asset. I also find mean-looking people far more interesting than not. And since my long legs would love to stretch straight out into the aisle from the center back seat, that only leaves me one choice: to the back of the bus I go.

I saunter toward the back with long, lanky strides and pick up some serious heavy-metal vibes from the rear. I hear someone humming an Aerosmith tune and can smell the familiar formaldehyde aroma of waste dissolver from the toilet. The dude—and I mean a classic, born-on-the-wrong-side-of-town, soaked-in-a-puddle-of-piss Dude—is somewhat reeking himself as he lies sprawled out, confident that he's got himself a private three-seat condominium. I guess him to be about thirty and life has treated him hard.

He feels me coming. He's twitching awake. His desert boots are full of holes, a Levi's jacket is pulled up to his ears, and his mustache hits his bottom lip. I can't see scars but I know he has them. I take a sniff of his three-week-old sweat, crusted and dried on his flaky white skin, smelling of highway rot and dirty road diesel. He's got on a Forty-Niners cap, the brim shadowing his eyebrows, and one good-sized bag, army green, is sitting at his feet because he's too fucking lazy to put it overhead. Either that or he's carrying drugs.

My guess is he's carrying, either speed or green bud.

I know it's going to be a tough sell to get him to share his seats. His eyes get bigger the closer I come. He doesn't know what to make of me. He jerks up a bit when it becomes obvious as a flash flood that I'm not here to bake a cake. Then I see the handle of a knife wrapped inside his jacket. I consider looking elsewhere, but that'd be admitting defeat. In a moment of inspiration I say, "I'll do you a favor. You let me have this outside seat here so I can stretch my long legs and I'll buy you something to eat at the next food stop."

He looks momentarily stunned in a three-day-binge sort of way. He has deep-set rheumy eyes and wiry eyebrows arched in ready defiance of anything I might have to say.

"I'll even buy you a steak!" I add, knowing full well that the last bus-stop steakhouse I'd seen was twenty years ago. That was in Oklahoma. We are a considerable distance from there.

Now I have him! I can see from the curl on his rotten mouth that he's not put a steak down for more than half a year and the prospect is tempting.

I feel a yes forming on his lips, but his eyes are so lost in steak reverie that for a moment I fear I've lost him to a trance. Finally he nods and his legs move enough off the aisle seat for me to sit down. I store my bag up above, settle into the seat next to the shitter and give my long legs a well deserved stretch. I can already feel him dissing me in his mind but I just smile, not a sick smile, but a smile, as genuine as it's going to get in the back of a Greyhound while in the middle of Oregon.

The bus roars off into rocky silence and I kiss Grants Pass goodbye.

Twenty tense miles down the road, headed toward

California, I sit watching heads, one by one, nod off into Greyhound slumberland. I wonder who on this rig has served time in federal penitentiaries.

My seatmate finally rustles from his frozen sprawl and mutters "Name's Rudy" in a voice so low it could choke a horse. He half extends his hand, full of calluses and highway sores. He sports a high school class ring.

I am shocked that he even talked at all. I suspect that isn't his real name, but I let it slide and stick out my bony hand. I suddenly feel like elaborating on my intense personal connection with the name Rudy.

"You know Rudolph was my dad's middle name. I always did like that name even if it was one of Santa's reindeer. And I knew this guy down in California named Rudy. I met him in a bar. He was going off about how he had a transistor radio installed in his brain and that his thoughts were monitored by the FBI. Well, I just finished up my beer, excused myself and walked home. But he followed. At first he was ten steps behind. Then he ran ahead, walked straight to my house and was waiting for me at the top of the stairs. I asked him how he knew I lived there. He just pointed to his head and said, 'The radio told me.' Anyhow, I like the name Rudy. My name's Michael, or Mike. Whatever."

The Rudy by my side is looking at me sort of crazy. He's attempting to pull himself up in his seat. I can see his hand resting under his jacket near the handle of his knife. He is staring at me like I'm the biggest loony that ever crossed his path, which could be slightly true on certain days.

"You a fag?" he finally utters.

I sit with this for a second while I consider what level

of denial I want to endure. Since I am on the outside seat, and in an odd sort of way feel safe to sprint, I decide to just throw in the goods and let him decide what to do with it.

"You know, that's a damn good question. Since we're going to be stuck together for the better part of this ride and since I can't help but notice you've got a little knife under your jacket, we might as well not play guessing games. Yes, I have walked that side of the fence if that's what you want to know. Now do *me* a favor and tell me what you're carrying in your bag."

I lean into him and motion down below his feet at his green bag. Things momentarily hang in midair.

"Fucking fag!" he mutters while shoving his duffel bag under his seat. He moves closer to the window, which is fine because I can use some space from his wretched stink.

Things stay like this for the longest time. By now we are pulling south, past Mt. Shasta. I am watching the shifting light of the day pull color off the top of the mountain and toss streamers of light across the highway. The day is giving up its brilliance. I can hear the drone of a voice from the front of the bus as the lady in the macramé vest rants on and on with the complete unabridged history of her health. This includes the most recent removal of an ovarian cyst that apparently had complications, enough so that she was peeing blood for a month and had to give up intercourse altogether. I can hear the driver intoning "Uh-huh, uh-huh" every few minutes just to keep the conversation alive.

Behind her I see the woman and daughter, the ones possibly on the lam, who are as nervous as ever. The mother has an unlit cigarette clamped between her teeth and is habitually stroking the girl's hair. At key moments in the conversation ahead she clasps her hands over the girl's ears as if to protect her from life's dirty secrets. Her face looks mildly familiar, like last week's broadcast of "America's Most Wanted." I start thinking about her plight and momentarily glance five seats behind her at the lone, good-looking white male who seems possibly psycho. He is munching from a bag of corn chips. He's attentively absorbing every word from the macramé lady while clutching his bag of chips. He silently feeds himself one chip at a time and almost chokes when she starts talking about the pus she found this morning on her sheets. The pus was a bright, almost canary yellow, and she wasn't sure if it was vaginal discharge or something even more disgusting. I cringe, and the good-looking white male is chewing his chips so deliberately my jaws hurt. She wrapped her discharge in a piece of tinfoil because she wanted to show it to a doctor in the city. For a fleeting moment, the good-looking white male, the mother and daughter possibly on the lam, a few monster-truck-rally types who've pricked up their ears to this fleeting conversation and I are all hoping by the love of Jesus that she isn't going to dig out the damn piece of tinfoil from her pink-and-white daisy-print clutch bag and show us the bright-as-canary yellow swab of pus that clung to her sheets in the early hours of the morning.

Thankfully she doesn't. We roll through California into the twilight.

My seatmate is coming to life, possibly from the sound of the slow mastication of corn chips ahead, and passes wind in my direction. Between the ovarian cyst, the smell of the toilet and him I feel momentarily faint but instead mutter, "What the hell did you have for lunch today?" as I fan the air in mock protest.

He likes that. The good old male bonding flatulence routine will get me a few miles of friendship in the back of this bus if I just don't mention the maggots that I think are living in his mustache.

"I'll tell you, this ride's made more stops than a whore full of bourbon," he suddenly rants as he clears his throat to spit on the floor.

Where this came from I don't know, but at least he's talking and I guess that's a sign that I'm now fit for his company. I feel a remote sense of belonging to the back-of-the-bus tribe. We're mean, we smell and the mere fact we're in the back makes us pals.

"And see that girl sitting up there. She's begging for it!" he points with his thumb.

I look up three rows at a fresh-faced girl of eighteen. Her hair is ratted with a wall of bangs a good four inches high. She wears a tight lacy tank top that barely covers her breasts and is a mess of pimples. I just know she's running from home.

I study her carefully and feel pity. I wonder what makes him feel so sure she's wanting it from him. Have they spoken a few words, or exchanged glances? Maybe she finds his sallow cheeks, crusty eyes and layers of spent denim a turn-on.

For the first time I think of him as a sexual object, which amuses me to the point that I'm almost snickering. I bet myself a cheap dollar I could seduce him before we hit the next county if I so choose. But I don't.

I pull out a flask.

I'm carrying my bottled spring water in a whiskey flask that my brother gave me years ago. It's small and silver with carefully etched designs and a tiny shot cap. It comes in handy when I don't want to take flak from dim-witted rednecks for sucking on a pint of Evian.

I like the furthered male bonding effect this has on my seatmate from...

"Where you from?" I ask.

"Arkansas."

"Me too." I'm impressed. That's one in a million. Either he's lying or we're next of kin.

"Well, damn." He too thinks I'm lying, but I'm not.

I don't care one bit that we're from the same state because I gave up on useless connections years ago.

I offer him a swig from my flask and don't let on that the only surprise in store is it's not whiskey. He accepts and hits off it with the vigor of a newborn. He doesn't seem even to notice that it's water. He smacks his lips and imagines a momentary rush of whiskey slipping down his dry throat. He sucks in some air like he's cooling his pipes.

If he can get high off of that...! I bet myself a quarter I could have him squealing on the floor by the time he finishes.

He starts ranting.

I suddenly dread this scene since I know he's a talker. I can just feel his story boiling inside. The more he drinks, the more he smacks like a bar bum in a hut. He's one shot away from blabbing his whole bloody story. I start slipping into his orbit. I know full well I'm going to hear the complete details of another sorry life from a red-faced loser in the back of the bus with nothing but trouble on his mind. I dig in my heels and stare straight ahead, ready for a sermon.

He hands me the empty flask, runs the tip of his pinkie across his overgrown bush of a mustache, shakes the last drop onto the floor and says, "Sorta weak." He shoves it on my lap, closes his eyes and begins to talk.

"Arkansas, huh? If you're from Arkansas, you're all right." He talks with a constant swirl of phlegm in the back of his throat and has me wishing I could clear it before he chokes.

"Listen to that old lady up front. She thinks she's got troubles. I'm in such a mess the devil wouldn't touch me if I begged." His speech is slurred. I feel like telling him there was nothing in the whiskey flask. But I keep quiet. I am tired of listening to the macramé lady and he's a good change.

"What mess are you in?" I ask, feeling without doubt I have released the lock to his room full of secrets. I settle in for the ride.

"I had a buddy that sort of looked like you, tall and skinny at least. His name was José but I called him Joe. Him and I met in Texas at the sheet-metal shop in Aberdeen where we worked. We were palling around, hanging by the Dumpsters every day after work, drinking quarts of Jack. He loved that shit.

"I never met anyone like him. He was never mean, never raised his voice at anyone. Everyone sort of liked him.

"Once or twice we scored a bag of junk and shot up at my place. I was living in this tiny shack outside of town. It used to be a chicken coop. We'd put on some music and get, like, totally messed up.

"Sometimes we'd both just nod off and I'd wake up with him holding me, like we're butt buddies or something. I'd push him away like, 'What the hell?' and we'd just laugh about it.

"Late winter I got laid off and wanted to get the hell

out of Texas. I wanted him to jump a train and come with me to Seattle, but he didn't want to get so far from his family. They lived in Mexico.

"One night before I left he came over and started crying like a woman. He's totally messed up, like we're never going to see each other. I was freaking, trying to make him stop. So I got out a big split of weed and lit up. He started telling me right in my face that he loved me. I'm saying 'You can't love me, I'm no woman.'

"He was wrestling me down, rolling on the floor, knocking shit around when he started coming onto me. Next thing you know we're groping at each other, our clothes come off and we just did it right there.

"The next day I left and we never said a word about it.

"Two months later I was in Seattle selling pot on the street. I was hanging out in Ballard and found this burnt-out squat near Eighty-fifth. A junkie was living there. I moved in. The first two rooms were burnt and boarded up, so we lived in the back.

"About that time I got a postcard from Joe saying he was coming to see me.

"Wasn't too long before he got there. He started living in the house with me and the other junkie. We were hurting for money, so we'd roam the streets at night collecting cans. Either that or I'd score a few bags and sell 'em down at Gasworks Park.

"One night Joe was bumming, big time. Like we were broke and hadn't partied in a while. He was thinking about his family and thinking he should of stayed in Texas. I was holding so I said, 'Let's party.' He's like, 'No way, you got to sell it,' and I was like, 'Come on, don't you want to party?'

"He finally gave in. We're in my room listening to Nirvana and tying off. I wanted to do the whole bag, so we hit up. It was really good shit. We were on the floor propped up against an old couch with candles burning and nodded out there, holding hands.

"When I came to the candles were burnt all the way down. My bones were aching from laying in one place so long. I looked over at Joe. He was all passed out with his mouth hanging open and drool running down his face. I pushed him with my foot to wake him up but he didn't move. I kicked him again but he just lay there, stiff. That's when I saw he wasn't breathing. I crawled over to him and forced his eyes open. They were gone man, like nothing was there. I felt for his heart, but it wasn't beating. That's when I freaked, big time. I started to yell at him to wake up. I was pinching his face and neck, punching him around and calling him names. Nothing was happening. I put my mouth on his mouth and started pumping air in his lungs. I kept at it for a long time, pounding on his chest, shaking his body back and forth. I slapped him once, good and hard. I wanted him so bad to open his eyes and quit playing this mind game with me... but there was nothing I could do.

"Joe was dead, man. He was dead.

"I just fell on top of him crying, like you know, he was my best friend. I just lay there talking to him, but he was gone.

"I finally got up and woke the other dude who lived there. He was like, 'Whatever, just get him the hell out of the house, man, or we're in for it big time.'

"I just wanted to beat the shit out of him.

"We got our shopping cart, the same one Joe and I used to collect cans. We crammed his body in it. His legs and arms were hanging off the sides. We wheeled him out of the house and onto the sidewalk.

"The other dude turned on his heels to go back in. I said, 'Where the fuck you going?' and he's like, 'It's your problem, man. You gave him the shit, now get rid of him!'

"I was out on the sidewalk in the early morning and no one was around. I kept thinking he was going to wake up any second, but he didn't. So I just wheeled him down the sidewalk about twenty blocks. I was just waiting for someone to spot me. But the streets were dead as Joe. I finally left him at a corner and gave him a kiss on the lips and could taste his death. It was bad, man. I left him there for some poor fuck to find on their morning jog.

"Back at the house I just grabbed my stuff. I took a few things of Joe's, you know, a shirt, his watch, a knife his favorite uncle gave him. I took his jean jacket. I don't know why. I was just taking mementos. I walked out of there with my green bag full of memories and got my ass down to the bus station. The sun was up, hitting the space needle, and I bought a ticket for Frisco, man. Like, shit, I don't know what I'm doing, I'm just running."

Rudy stops talking for a while and I feel like I haven't taken a breath in hours. I am leaning hard on my elbow and my ear is within an inch of his mouth. The night has swallowed us whole, and no one else on the bus is awake except the macramé lady, who is still ranting to the driver about an auto accident she had at the age of twenty and the broken collarbone that took three months to heal.

I look over at Rudy and his face is redder than ever. I think I see a trace of a tear slipping down his stubbled cheek. He turns to look out the wall of glass at the stream of trucks going the other direction. I hesitate a moment before taking his hand.

"You mean this just happened this morning?" I ask.

"Yeah, dude, you got it!"

"Aren't you afraid they'll find you?"

"Hey, I don't give a shit. I just want Joe back. I blew it, man. I blew it big time. I just want him back from wherever he's gone. I know one thing, though. I'm going clean, man. I am never, never touching shit again. Never!"

Rudy pushes away my hand. We sit in the back of the bus with the diesel roar of the engine sounding louder than ever. The stink of the toilet nearby has nearly evaporated beneath his story. The constant drone of the macramé lady feels like a backdrop for a more rueful life than any boarder on this bus could ever bear.

We ride forward into the night, saying nothing.

At Sacramento I go looking for a steakhouse for Rudy, but it's one-thirty in the morning. Rudy says anything will do. He doesn't want to get out of the bus and stays in the back. His green bag is firmly stored beneath his feet and Joe's jacket is pulled up to his mustache. I wander the streets of Sacramento. I finally settle on a Big Mac and fries for Rudy. For a second I contemplate filling my flask with real whiskey but don't.

Rudy is sleeping when I return and the final leg to San Francisco has everyone snoring on board. Even the macramé lady has finally run out of maladies to share. The mother and daughter have at last fallen into peaceful slumber. The single white male who is possibly psycho clutches his consumed bag of corn chips. The girl with the bangs has curled into sleep.

And this dirty dog of a Greyhound delivers us all like a band of fugitives to the waiting Bay Area.

3

Art and Money, God and Sex

San Francisco rolls out its wet, soggy carpet and pulls me from the bus terminal at seven in the morning. Rudy's out of here before I can even offer advice and gives me no hope that we'll ever cross paths again.

I give Annie Sprinkle a call in New York and let her know I'll soon be on my way. I can feel her sexy smile three thousand miles away.

Outside, the streets are already busy with the electric whir of Muni buses discharging commuters into the high-rise grid. Plummeting through traffic, I race up Market for Geary Street. I catch a bus to Japantown, searching in my tired address book for my good friend Viktor. I've been getting wild, frantic messages from him and want to see what's going on before I head east. I jump out near Fillmore and search for Viktor's flat. Having no street number to go by, I am hoping memory will serve me. Of the hundreds of doors on Sutter Street one in particular finally screams out so loud I can't possibly miss it. It is a silver-splattered door with a pink bra and a high-heeled shoe tacked above the bell. The door is ajar. After several

unanswered rings I cautiously step inside to what I assume
to be the home of my old friend Viktor Fidele.

Inside the flat are hundreds of balloons—looks like a
party. The balloons stink a bit in that rubbery sort of way.
I stand in the middle of one room and look at a plastic
sculpture hanging from the ceiling. It's draped in white
fabric and turns a slow circle like a ghost in mid-flight.

Viktor is nowhere to be found. But his art is
everywhere.

The dimly lit room contains half a dozen mannequins dressed in costumes and wearing wigs. I now know
this is the place. Vik goes nowhere without his
mannequins.

He's here, I just know it, I think to myself. *I can smell him.
He's in here somewhere, probably watching me.*

Suddenly Viktor bursts from the next room through
a curtain of ribbons, smoking a cigarette and carrying a
tape measure in his hand.

He is talking to himself: "There's never enough light,
never enough light in this place. I'm going blind," he
rants while poking through the balloons, oblivious to my
presence.

"Michael...*Michael*!" He suddenly stops in his tracks
when he realizes I'm standing but a cat's breath away. "Oh,
I'm so glad to see you. When did you get here?"

"Just this moment," I say, giving him a big, juicy hug.

Viktor puts down his cigarette, clears away a few
balloons and takes a good look at me. "Oh, love your head!
Who shaved you?"

"I did. I shaved it in Oregon before heading to the
city."

Viktor steps back. "You've been gone. Where've you
been?"

"Viktor—I've been gone for years. Remember? I called to say goodbye but your phone was disconnected. I heard you've been trying to find me." I stepped toward him. "Are you okay? Tell me what's going on."

"Do you know how to sew a French seam?" he asks me.

"What?"

"A French seam. Do you know how to sew one?"

"Uh, sure. Why?"

"Well, that's all that matters. Come, come. See my new line. It's my latest collection. Something for everyone."

I stop him in his tracks. "Wait a second Viktor, what's going on? Why have you been wanting to see me?"

"Because I missed you. That's why. And besides, I need you."

"Sure, I missed you, too. But what's up?"

Viktor retrieves his smoke and leads me by the hand out the room, toward the back. "Oh, I'm a nervous wreck. I've got a show coming up and I don't have enough models. I need more models, but my gowns aren't fitting. It's très petit for everyone. My entire line is too tight. Why is everyone so *big*? They've been working at the gym too long, that's why. Look at you. You're thin. You're beautiful. You're here. That's all that matters. You'll be a model? *Mais oui*?"

"Model? You want me to model? Viktor, are you out of your mind? I've got to get to the East coast by Thursday. Is this why you've been calling? I thought something was seriously wrong."

"But something was seriously wrong. My heart's been aching to see you. And besides, now that you're here you can model for me. The mini-shift. It's made for you."

"Viktor you're out...of...your...mind!" I laugh and we traipse through the flat, kicking through piles of fabric and debris.

Viktor lives amid squalor and always has. As we walk through the halls, passing crayon art, hanging sculptures and clusters of balloons, I feel like I'm looking through a kaleidoscope. Posters hang on the walls alongside signature portraits of friends. Street trash, glued and varnished, hangs from the ceilings. Everywhere we turn art screams for attention.

"So, Viktor, tell me what's been going on. You're obviously still designing."

"I'll never stop. I've been dreaming most of my latest designs. And the materials I use are so cheap. In fact, they're free. Absolutely free. I get them out of alleys and South-of-Market industrial Dumpsters. Can you believe they throw this out?"

I cautiously walk through the fitting room toward a back closet. Viktor's designs are hanging against the wall. I stand there, surveying racks of costumes in the dark corner.

"So this is it?" I say with my arms crossed.

Viktor blows smoke rings with an expectant glare. "What do you think?"

I squint and try to make sense of what I see. "It looks like rubber body suits with aluminum piping. And maybe nylon rope laced over sheet metal. I don't know. What is it?"

"They're monuments!" he yells. "They aren't clothing, they're monuments!"

"Are they wearable?"

Viktor nods. "Well, sort of. Maybe not by ordinary people. I'm designing for royalty."

"Royalty?"

"Well, royalty of the subconscious!"

I stand with a blank look on my face. But a friend's a friend. So I wholeheartedly laud his creations with a round of applause, knowing I'll figure it out before the day is through.

A look around the room reveals a shocking array of designs. What I take to be a bowl of pistachios turns out to be a hat. And when I start to sit in a comfy-looking chair, Viktor pulls me away from sitting on what is his newest gown. I quickly learn that what appears to be furniture or table settings was actually worn last evening.

After half an hour of looking at his collection, I finally beg the inevitable. "Viktor, which is the front? And which end is up?" I ask, holding a dress.

"You know, that's one of the most often asked questions about my work. I don't really have a good answer yet. It's something I've been working on, though."

"Well, I wish you luck," I snicker.

We spend another half hour talking about our lives before he finally brings me back to the subject of modeling.

"So, what are you doing tonight? You've arrived just in time. I'm doing a *très* fab showing of my latest collection and you *must* be there to model. You'll do it, *mais oui?*"

"You're not kidding? You really want me to model for you?" Somehow I can't see myself doing anything of the kind.

"Come on. You're in town. Let's have fun!"

"Why not?" I finally shrug.

Vik and I spend most of the day together carousing on upper Market, drooling over chocolates and men. We spend an hour at Cafe Flore, critiquing hair, and another hour at Walgreens, handing out flyers for the evening's spectacle. At sunset we trudge over to Fillmore, pick up the costumes and then take a cab to Hayes Valley. We arrive at the large flat where a friend is hosting the fashion show. A crowd of models is waiting at the bottom of the steps.

Viktor herds us up the stairs and into the flat like schoolchildren late for class.

"These are what you would call assorted-sized models," he whispers as we ascend. "I like to go for realism, not vanity."

The models are not very model-like. We're a ragged crew of varying heights and shapes, with more than one of us packing a healthy gut. The muscle queens stand on one side of the room and the portly ones stand on the other. I'm the only skinny one of the bunch and stand alone.

Finally Viktor unravels a dozen plastic garment bags and drapes the outfits over a piano. We start picking through them like we're at a backyard rummage sale.

"Please, please!" Viktor claps his hands. "A little dignity. I have assignments for all of you. Just wait your turn."

I stand back, not sure if I can possibly adapt my six-foot-three frame, no matter how thin, into anything that I see floating around the room.

"The basic rule is not to worry whether it fits, but to take care not to scrape off the wallpaper when we walk down the halls. Anthony will be very annoyed. He just had it redone."

There is more metal incorporated into his designs than found on a tank. I immediately sense the danger of wearing one of his monuments and wish I had forgone this experience. But it was too late now.

"Michael, here's your mini-shift. It's made of the finest plastic bubble wrap. Hinge it closed with these three-foot strips of aluminum tubing. The waist belts nicely with this ten-foot band of Diet Pepsi pop-tops and the shoulders are quilted with foot-deep foam. Now those are the king of shoulder pads, are they not?"

Despite the fact that it is now spring, this is a special showing of Viktor's long-awaited winter collection.

We spend close to an hour pulling ourselves into our second skins while Viktor busies himself with the time-honored last-minute task of repairing ripped seams. After a brief rehearsal and lots of glue and staples, the doors are finally opened.

The waiting guests are all too happy to come in from the cool, foggy street below. They are escorted through the flat, down the stairwell and out to the patio out behind the building. There they are treated to a healthy bowl of knock-you-on-your-butt fruit punch. It's a well coiffed crowd, considering this is San Francisco. Once the guests are thoroughly soused, Viktor introduces the show with a medley of songs that I do not know—and I am not the only one. In a fit of harmonic tension, we stumble through the medley in such discord that the neighborhood dogs start caroling.

The guests don't seem to mind. They swoon at our musical renditions. Halfway through, a rumor spreads that the punch might be psychedelic. And from the plastered grins on nearly every face, I tend to believe it.

Viktor finally holds up his hand with a nervous quiver and silences the chorus to make an announcement.

"Ladies and gentlemen, welcome to the third annual showing of my winter collection. I hope that you've all brought your pocketbooks and wallets. In a short while we will begin the show. But I've heard we're about to have some stormy weather and I'm so, so sorry but you just might get wet."

Smiling, grinning faces look up from the courtyard. Glasses of punch clink in toasts as guests murmur among themselves.

Two roughish characters unravel a garden hose from the side of the wall. The unsuspecting guests are suddenly sprayed down by a jet of water until everyone is soaking wet, with the exception of the models, of course.

The guests are running in all directions, trying to take cover under tables, lawn chairs and trees, but to no avail. Everyone is drenched down to their underwear.

As the pleading crowd is escorted back inside, its options are to go home, stay for the evening in soggy attire or don the most fashionable costumes from Viktor's collection.

"Sales always shoot sky-high with our stormy-weather segment," Viktor whispers to me. "I'm so surprised Macy's hasn't used the technique. Almost everyone buys a dry change of clothes. I mean, after all, it's the only fashionable thing to do."

But there are only a few purchasers. Most of the wise-ass crowd seem perfectly content to slosh their way up the stairs, sit in their clammy clothes, sip punch and grin ear to ear.

When all have been seated in the packed living room at the front of the flat, Viktor enters from the parlor announcing in his nasal best, "The theme of this year's

winter extravaganza is Art and Money, God and Sex. I
want everyone to repeat after me: Art and Money, God
and Sex."

"Art and Money, God and Sex," the dripping crowd
chants, having no idea how this relates to fashion.

Then, as the show begins, Viktor narrates the outfits.
He keeps us on cue while putting out the fires ignited by
gowns meeting the flames of candles. Meanwhile, backstage hysteria mounts. The models frantically try to
disrobe and climb into tighter outfits. So tight even I can't
fit.

Muzak plays over the stereo. The models waltz in a
continuous stream from the back dressing room through
the mile-long hall and across the runway floor toward the
living room.

Nearly a hundred guests hold on to their wallets as
each riveting fashion statement sweeps the room to an
overwhelming response. They are not sure what they are
looking at and neither are we.

"Which is the pantaloons and which is the gown?"
one model screams from the changing room.

"Which is the belt and which is the shoe, Viktor?"
yells another.

Viktor is perfectly poised, ignoring the confusion
from his assorted-sized models and continuing his narra-
tion. "Lawrence is wearing an exquisitely conceived
piped-lamé standing collar...with matching plastic
ruffled cuffs..."

"And Monique is wearing a perforated industrial-
rubber vest..."

Backstage there is great confusion in distinguishing
petticoats from hats. Suddenly a fitting-room brawl

breaks out when two large models start suffocating in their rubber rainwear.

One girl is holding in her own rolls of flesh that have been forced out the top of her cinched waist. She screams as the zipper jaws of her aluminum vest threaten to turn her into mincemeat.

My hands are beginning to turn a deep shade of blue from the constricted cuffs on my fashionable coat. I don't mind, since it's all for love of a friend. But when the razor-sharp edges of my belt begin threatening to severe me in half, I barely stop myself from screaming.

Viktor ushers us through without even a nod to our pain. The guests are by now a mass of grins, their eyes open wide. I feel like the punch has taken its toll. They sit in their stupors, absorbing this flight of fashion while we shred the walls.

The finale of the show comes not a moment too soon. Our tender flesh can barely endure another round. It's time for the black-and-white evening attire with Viktor's prized size-six number that he has held in reserve for me.

I stand in the back with three pairs of hands helping me to pull on a piece so tight my ribs fold in half. It takes two sets of pliers and vise grips to close me in. If I could breathe I would. I hobble down the hall, hoping for the best.

Viktor is pleased at the transformation of my manly anatomy. I look more like a praying mantis than a fashion model.

As I enter the room, the back row of guests rises to get a better view.

Viktor announces in a worn runway voice, "Ladies and gentlemen, here is *la pièce de résistance*, our flared, over-the-shoulder, high-end, hand-fastened French maid skirt made of perforated industrial rubber, coat hangers and a dangerously tight aluminum bodice laced with metal spikes. Doesn't his bright pink puckered flesh look absolutely alarming? The industrial rubber guarantees to hold up in the most compromising positions."

And right on cue, I bend over to show the industrial strength of his rubber garments but am humiliated as my bare bottom rips through the seam for everyone to see.

Viktor is alarmed but the guests are very pleased.

I run off the stage.

The models are packed into the hall, awaiting curtain call, when I charge for the changing room, begging for a breath of air. I hold my bare bottom, trip over a light fixture, plow into a water cooler and cause half the cast of models to fall like a set of dominoes.

The house is in a sudden uproar. Guests run down the hall, tearing through the writhing models on the floor. I can hear bubble wrap popping and jagged pop-top belts crunching like broken bones.

I hold the loose light fixture in my hand. The electricity suddenly goes out. Someone yells "Earth-quake!" and the flat empties in a mad stampede for the street, leaving strips of rubber trailing down the steps. Guests hit the pavement, clutching their pocketbooks and smiling wide plastic smiles.

And Viktor is out there trying to close sales.

"All sales are final! All sales are final! Don't forget: Art and Money, God and Sex.

"Fashion is sex. Sex is fashion. If you can't say sex, you can't be fashionable!"

But the crowd drifts down the street to a block party that will put a quick end to this show.

Viktor walks back to the flat, letting out a telling sigh.

I loosen myself from my restraints, suck in a breath of air and ask optimistically, "So Viktor, was the show a success?"

"*Mais oui.* A few sales. But everyone complains. They say I make antifashion. That my fashion hurts. Can you imagine? I say, no pain, no fashion! Fashion is painful or it isn't working."

And once again I have to ask, "Which end is up?"

4

The Man With No Penis

Monday morning I bid Vik goodbye. I look at the map and study the miles to New York, wondering just how I'm going to get there in four days.

I call down to the drive-away agency, but the only car going east is bound for Nashville. The closest I'd ever been to Nashville was Memphis, the most miserable city I've ever lived in. I was only nine then. It was 1959 and water fountains were marked "colored" or "white." Like other little white boys, I was kept by a black ironing maid while my mom did the shopping. But that's history now.

I say no to Nashville and call back an hour later. This time they have a car going all the way to Patterson, New Jersey. That's close enough for me. I do somersaults on Market Street, I'm so happy.

The drive-away car is a funky-looking red-and-white Toyota Tercel. It has a dented left rear fender, a severely faded Clinton-Gore bumper sticker and an FM that doesn't work. That will leave me with a long stretch of AM listening, which means hours' worth of country music if I'm lucky enough to find even that on the dial.

It's a good day for a drive. The roads are clear and I'll be glad to get out from underneath the Frisco fog belt. I can already feel the cascade of sunlight on my cheeks. The car has a sun roof, so I open it all the way while I gas her up on the corner of Brannan and Third. I mark a rough line on the map between here and New Jersey.

Heading over the Bay Bridge, I throw Vik a kiss and pat my little Tercel on the dash. This good little car better be nicer than the last. I check out the backseat knowing full well I am going to have to cram myself there to sleep tonight.

Across the bridge I feel like splurging on a meal and pull into Berkeley for some long-lasting nutrition. This time I get myself a *dozen* bean-and-cheese burritos at the Taco Bell before hitting the open road. These burritos store just fine in the glove compartment. Whatever they put in them just keeps forever. I'll need that for the long ride ahead.

I hit Interstate 80 about eleven in the morning. I decide to push the speedometer up to eighty on I-80. This becomes my mantra and lasts all the way to Cheyenne. I'm ready to leave this mess of a West coast and make a trail across America.

The California sun is beating down on my head. I reach in my bag for a bottle of the highest number sunblock known to mankind. I'm not about to put a hat on top of this shiny skull of mine. That would keep the wind from blowing the few spikes of hair I have.

I skirt through Sacramento past miles of nut or-chards and across the Sacramento Valley. It's blazing under the spring sun. Rice fields are burning and irriga-tion ditches are filled to the brink, flooding the fruit and nut basket of the West. I see stretches of land racing to the hills, cultivated and broken by the industrial plow, sprayed and pruned. High-tech wars waged every day against insect and disease. I swear enough food grows here to feed the world.

I scream like a maniac, happy as a bird to be soaring again down the interstate and heading east for the Big A. This highway's okay as long as I don't get a flat. I plan not to stop until I've run out of gas or see a thumb on the side of the road.

No sooner than I think that, I see it. The man with the thumb is standing on the side of the freeway past the signs that say NO PEDESTRIANS. I've driven by him in a flash but I remember my motto—"Pick up the first thumb, the engine will hum"—and I swerve to a stop. I check in the rearview mirror to see whether this is going to be trouble from the start or trouble down the road.

He's a young guy in baggy jeans and a denim shirt, with long brown hair, nearly to his shoulders, parted in the middle. With no hesitation, I peg him for a Deadhead. Then I see he's got a suitcase, not a backpack, and a bright look on his brow. I thank God he doesn't have a dog waiting in the ditch or a hidden tribe waiting across the road. He's blistering from the sun. I tell him to hop on in because he's my lucky charm for getting across the desert.

I bet myself his name is Chris. He just looks like one. But if he calls me "dude" within five miles the deal's off and he's out of here. I don't need another dude around after four hundred miles with Rudy on the bus.

He gets in and we pass the awkward moment when both the rider and the driver are making two-second assessments as to whether the other is a potential serial killer. The moment is tense. We mask it under questions that any fifth grader would ask.

So I say, "Where you headed?" because if he asks me first then I'm left unarmed with information.

He one-ups me and says, "As far as you're headed."

This leaves me in the dark. Now I know he's either running from the law or headed all the way to the East coast.

"Well, we'll just see how far I get, 'cause this isn't my car." I figure I've been vague enough to stall for time. I can get in his head and he in mine before we decide to do a long haul.

He doesn't stink and that's a good sign. His suitcase, however funky and old, is like the kind you buy from a Goodwill store when you suddenly need to take a trip and never owned luggage in your life. It's a spiffy Samsonite piece with a silver bar and a mess of stickers on it, like it's been around the world a few times.

His suitcase settled on the backseat, he firmly shuts the door, and my God if he isn't a bright-as-a-new-pony, smooth-faced man with clean teeth and a big canyon smile that could blind a nun from a mile away. I toss out my Deadhead theory.

I surmise he's either a born-again Christian or he's had one hell of a life and is just that much more grateful than the rest of us to be living on the road.

"Name's Chris," he says.

I high-five myself for intuition and introduce myself with the same line I've used on the road for over two hundred thousand miles: "Name's Michael or Mike. Whatever."

It sets a familiar mood. He pulls on his seatbelt in eager readiness for the trip ahead. But not before he pulls an open bottle of spring water out of the back and offers me a swig.

I decide I'll like him, smile and all. I don't give a flying Jesus if he is with the Lord, I just know he doesn't have a gun. And from the feel of his grip as I shake his hand, I know I could beat him down to the ground if he turns psycho by the time we get to Nevada.

Off we roar, doing eighty on I-80 through Donner Pass. He starts whistling a sweet tune like my dad used to do.

We head down from the mountains. I'm chewing on my seventh burrito and offer him one, knowing full well he'll take it. He does. He opens up the burrito and eats out the insides, cheese and beans, then tosses out the soggy tortilla, which I admit is kind of pathetic. He licks his lips like a cow on a salt block and flashes me another grin.

He's got me in the palm of his hand, this one has.

We're talking about the White House, pulling punches at the Democrats and going on like we know what's good for the whole country. He's got a voice like warm milk and practically floats off his seat, he's so glad I gave him a ride. He's a lanky one, like me, and has on a pair of boots that look like he's worked the dirt. He smells like a campfire, or sage on the open prairie. I notice hints of the woods clinging to his blue denim shirt.

We're talking, driving, finishing off another burrito and hitting Nevada near Reno when I think I hear him say, "I got no prick," in between sentences, but it slides right over me.

We're swapping stories about the perils of the road, comparing the longest time we've waited for a ride. Chris is carrying on with some wild tales, laughing like a loon. I laugh at his laugh. Things are looking good.

I pull off at Reno. I remember this slot machine that's like an old friend. I've got a score to settle. Years ago on my first trip through I was cruising the casinos. I came across this one little bank of dollar slots in the far back of Harvey's. I'd only put in two silver dollars when I hit a two hundred-dollar jackpot out of the bucket.

Ever since then, I stop and say hello to that little slot machine whenever I pass through. Sometimes she's taking from me and sometimes she gives. But she's been winning the past few years. So out of habit I pull up to Harvey's. Chris and I march in. He's into it.

I walk straight to the change booth and break a five. I find my slot machine sitting unused toward the back, near the crap tables, and drop in the coins. I lose four times in a row. But the fifth hits a small win. I'm out of there twenty dollars richer, which is fine. My luck's changing and that's all I need to know.

We're back on the road. I had noticed Chris walking with a walk, not a limp or a hobble, but just a funny walk. I study him in the car and we speed toward Winemucca. He shows me a book he's reading. I can see his legs bouncing with each word.

"You nervous or something? What's up with you?" I finally ask. Somehow I know that's the fatal question. Everyone waits for someone with a face like mine that begs to hear the deep dirty secrets they've been harboring inside.

"I'm bleeding," he says after a long silence. He starts whistling songs as he flips through the pages of the book he's reading.

"Bleeding?"

"Yeah, bleeding. Just a little. Sort of from my penis, except I don't have one."

I do not make sense of this.

"Like, are you cut, or what do you mean?"

"I'm, like, bleeding, Mike. I cut off my dick."

"You cut off your dick?" I twitch in my seat, a primordial twitch. We're still doing eighty on I-80 in the cocoon of the car, full of a dozen burritos, and this sweet man with the face of an angel is telling me what?

"What do you mean, you cut off your dick?" My eyes drift down to where I'd imagine the object of discussion to be if it were there. I find myself wanting to pull over, call it a night and wish him well.

"Hey, don't worry, I'm not, like, talking about a major hemorrhage at this point." He let it be, as if that's all there was to it.

For a moment I consider dropping the subject, but it wasn't going away. "So, you've got a little cut?"

"No, I don't have a little cut. It's like this, Mike, I cut off my penis last winter. Like, really cut it off with a knife. Sometimes I get a little blood if the scar rubs on my zipper."

I'm cringing in my driver's seat. My legs are drawn together. My mind does a tailspin as I battle the impulse to feel sympathetic pain for such a story as his. *Penis? A knife?* I can't quite match the action with the man sitting next to me. He looks anything but a penis mutilator.

"Uh, listen. You're okay? Like, do we need to get you to a doctor?"

"No, it's cool. It'll stop."

"Cool?" I can't imagine anything *cool* about this.

"Yeah, don't worry. It's just what happened last winter. It's a long story if you want to hear."

I slowly turn my head away from him toward my door window and look at my reflection. A slow, incredulous smile creeps across my face. I realize I must be the most unrepentant voyeur that God ever made because I would no more not want to hear his story than a fish would not want to be in water.

I turn to him again, trying not to sound patronizing, and I say, "Sure, go ahead. What happened?" I know this time I'm really in for a ride. We've got a lot of miles ahead.

"Well," he begins, "I was going to college in Portland, Maine, and moved in with this girl. She was different. I mean, she was on this whole death trip, collecting dead things, like rats, lizards, birds. She was, like, into the occult.

"When I was a senior we met this old lady, Helen, north of Portland, who lived on a boat. It was docked on the bay and she'd lived there forever. It was, like, the most decrepit, old rotting thing afloat.

"We'd go over there and Helen would always pull down the shades and light these stinking candles. Her place was like a vision of hell. It was stacked to the roof with old junk.

"Whenever we'd come over she'd put me in another room. She and Claudia would get off on doing really, really weird shit. I mean, like, she'd bring in a live chicken, slit its throat and gut it on her floor. She'd go wild, she was so into blood. She'd light fires right on the floor. She and Claudia would spend hours burning crumpled up paper with names on it.

"After a year of hanging with Helen, Claudia and I were barely connected. We'd long stopped having sex and she didn't give a shit about school. After I graduated we were over at Helen's all the time. They were inseparable. By late fall I was really getting tired of it. I wanted to go back to L.A. for Christmas to see my dad. I wanted her to go with me.

"But she wasn't into it at all. She wouldn't leave Helen and didn't want me to leave her.

"One night Helen gave me these coins. One was Haitian and it was double-headed. The other was just a U.S. silver dollar minted the year I was born. She said to keep them with me and when in doubt to just flip the silver dollar—'Heads you do it, tails you don't.'

"About a week before Christmas we were at the boat and Helen was in a wicked mood. We were sitting there in her freezing boat, huddled around her small heater, when she went off into one of her fits. Helen wanted me to cut my thigh and put out some blood. I was like, 'No way.'

"She held out her knife, this really twisted piece with an ivory handle. I was flipping, I couldn't believe she wanted me to do this. They both started mocking me, like, chanting 'Cut it, cut it, cut it.' They had totally evil looks on their faces. I finally just blew them off and hurled the knife against the wall as hard as I could. It cracked a vase on a shelf with this sick-looking skull inside. It crashed to the floor. Helen flipped on me. Claudia was right there too, close to thrashing me. I kicked my way out of the house, left Claudia, got in my van and drove back to town. I didn't waste time. I just packed my things in the van and left Maine that night, heading west for L.A. I was sick of them.

"I don't know how I did it. I stayed on the freeway and drove like a demon for days. But I started crashing bad near El Paso. I finally stopped early in the morning, the day before Christmas. I found this really sleazy motel on the outskirts of town. It was a total dump, with a dirt parking lot and a long row of rooms with kitchenettes that were barely safe to walk in. The place was full of people who lived there by the month. I paid ten dollars for a night and crashed out really bad. I wanted to sleep forever.

"So I woke up twenty-four hours later on Christmas day in this wretched room. The place was a hellhole. I wandered around the room stepping on roaches and puking in the sink. I put these two coins Helen had given me on a table and walked outside into the courtyard. The sun had barely come up. This Mexican whore in the farthest room was just coming in from the night. She began coming on to me. I was not into it at all. She was taunting me with this wicked smile and told me I'd better use it or I'd lose it. She was cackling with this really sick laugh.

"These two Mexican men pulled up and they knew her. They got out of their car and both had on the same belt, with a matador holding a sword embossed on the buckle. They were all chattering. I went back to my room and shut the door, listening to them. They were calling me a pussy. I walked over to the table. I could still hear her saying 'Use it or lose it.'

The two-headed coin was there on the table. I could hear Helen and Claudia in my head, chanting 'Cut it, cut it,' just like they did on the boat.

"The whore was still yelling 'Use it or lose it' and something went wrong in me. These symbols started floating through my head. All of this had a sudden deep significance. I was going off into this confused space and felt like a puppet. I looked at myself in the mirror and was disgusted for being a man. Suddenly I dropped my pants to the floor and was standing there looking at my penis. It seemed so revolting to me. It had been so long since I'd had sex. It was just like this awful, shriveled appendage hanging off me.

"It was Christmas and my mind was scrambled. My head was full of voices and everything became a symbol. I reached for a kitchen knife that was lying on the table. I took the silver dollar and tossed it up really hard. It landed heads-up on the table. I looked at the coins and the knife, heard the voices and suddenly I got this clear message. There was no longer any question what I should do. I grabbed my penis and pulled at it. I took the knife and sliced right through, as quick as I could, in one ragged cut.

"I was, like, standing there bleeding bad all over the place. I was holding my penis in my hand. I walked to the door with my pants down to my ankles. I hobbled out the door to the next room. I banged on the door and a short, fat, Mexican man who had drank through the night opened the door. I said to him, 'Excuse me, I just cut off my penis and I'm bleeding. Can you call a doctor?' And I passed out at his feet."

Chris and I, in the Toyota, are still cruising eighty on I-80. My hands hold the wheel so tight my knuckles are white and bloodless. My unblinking eyes match my ears, straining to hear every word. I'm not sure if I'm breathing. Chris is tapping his foot anxiously to the cadence of his words. I have not moved a muscle for miles. It's dark and the night doesn't scare me, but the thought of day does. I calculate the minutes before sunrise. I think how forbidden sleep seems and think what a war zone life can be.

"Then what happened?" I ask somberly.

"I don't know, I guess I bled a lot and they got me to a hospital. There was only a skeleton crew there. They didn't even try to sew it back on. I was put in a mental hospital for three months in El Paso. My dad flew out to see me once. He totally couldn't handle it. He was like

cardboard the whole time. He treated me like I was in for
a broken leg. It was cold, man.

"So I was with this really pathetic shrink. He was
totally clueless what to do with me. He was so patronizing—an overzealous young father from Albuquerque who
was stuck on protocol and basic Freudian 101. He watched
me like a hawk every day. It was the same question
morning and night, 'Anything new you'd like to share?'

"'Yeah, like I think it grew another inch today,' I'd
say. He had no sense of humor. None.

"He had me diagnosed totally by the book. I just
kissed his ass until he thought I was adjusted and signed
my release. What a joke.

"I took money out of my trust fund and hit the road
again. I sold my van because I'd lost my license and took
the train to L.A. for a week to see Dad. But he was
heartless. He thought I should be committed."

Chris pauses for a second and takes a deep breath.

"All I want, all I really want right now is to find
Claudia. I don't know what that means, but I want to know
what they were doing with me. I'm going back to Maine.
That's where I'm heading."

At the next town, on the border of Utah, we stop for
gas. For the first time in hours I realize I'm a person, not
just a confessional on wheels. I can't quit thinking of the
motel in El Paso, the coins, the knife, the matador belts
and the whole scene on the boat with the old woman, her
hens and the piles of junk.

Suddenly I say, "Do you still have the two-headed
coin?"

He digs through his pocket and produces the coin,
rubbed, worn and about the size of a quarter with the

head of a man on each side. He flips it over and over so I can see.

"You really did this, cut off your penis?" I ask a bit skeptically.

Chris is not a bit reticent in showing me what remains of his penis in the men's room at the Texaco while we're taking a pee. I look at his stump of manhood, no more than a puckered knob of flesh. I mentally make note to never, ever come near a knife while feeling manic on a Christmas day.

5

Long Roads and Tall Hats

A pair of long, tall boots with silver tips on the end stand at the door. I'm looking at them through the slit of one crusted eye, tracing the red stitching that falls in cloverleaves around the arch. I see dirt, pavement, dog shit and a man looking down at me with what I can't decide is a smile or a frown.

Fast-moving diesels are churning the air awake on the freeway. I feel my own slobber running down my face and neck into my arm pit. If my legs were anywhere to be found, I might get up and greet the stranger. But I'm in a twisted mess in the backseat of the car with both doors open wide.

I can feel my left arm beneath me and totally useless. My right hand is wrapped through a seatbelt sticking beneath the driver's seat. For a second I don't think I'm wearing pants, either, which turns out to be true. I'm not.

I'm in my boxers. God only knows where I am or who this is.

"Hey, can you move it? You're blocking us, asshole." As it turns out, the now-frowning face is not a man's but from someone who looks like a man with the voice of a woman.

I don't respond and she rocks the car like she's rocking a boat. "Come on, you're blocking us. Move it, please!"

The please gets me up.

I look out the door. Indeed I am blocking the back of a blue pickup camper. Now there are two of them standing outside.

"Yeah, yeah," I sort of grunt.

They study me a moment too long. I know I look a mess, with my coat balled up under my head and mean-looking whiskers growing off my chin. But it's the road and I forgive it.

I finally say, "All right."

They turn, satisfied enough that I'll be moving soon.

I don't know if it's morning or afternoon. I sit up and bump my head for the two millionth time. I stare toward the front of the car and see an arm and a sleeping body. But in my yet-to-be-awakened state I don't register or care who it is. Suddenly Chris pops up and we're looking eye to eye.

"I thought you left!" I'm sorry I said it, but it's the truth. I thought I'd let him off down the road when his story got so psycho on me. I feel this dread as the details come flooding back in.

He smiles his deep canyon smile and reminds me that he offered to pay the gas all the way to Jersey. Apparently we'd struck a deal in the early hours of dawn, and here he is, penis and all. Or no penis and all.

"You sleep good?" he's asking me.

"That's a pathetic question to ask a six-foot-three giant in the back of a Toyota Tercel. No, I didn't sleep good. I just closed my eyes and let nature do its damage. How 'bout you?"

"I slept pretty solid. I like the smell of cars."

"The smell of cars? What's that got to do with sleep?"

"They just smell sexy. It puts me to sleep."

I make a mental note to explore this smell thing further.

We unravel ourselves and step out of the car. I feel pressure from the nearby campers to step on it, so I do. They're angrily waiting. I know they're dykes because they've got a saphhic sister sticker on the back of their camper.

"What state are we in?" I holler as I pull myself into a pair of pants that are tight as a girdle. I toss them off for an oversized pair that are too loose. I finally settle for the same blue shorts I've worn for days.

The tall woman in a black hat whose boots I was studying earlier says, "Utah, land of the Mormons. Better watch yourself! Now hurry up before I push this little piece of crap out of the way myself."

Chris is struggling to put on his work boots. He has such a charm about him that I imagine anyone would like him. He asks them where they're going and they say they are headed to the march on Washington. I am not too surprised.

For a fleeting moment I entertain the notion of taking a ride all the way with them and letting Chris have the drive-away. But the look in their eyes says "We're in a totally dysfunctional relationship and we're taking this trip to try to recreate the magic we once shared."

I dutifully keep my mouth shut.

They like Chris but not me. I begin to wonder if he qualifies as a eunuch. If this is proof that androgyny is the solution to the world's problems, then what a better place it'd be if we were all sexless humans with nothing but goodness in our hearts.

Oh my god, what a thought. I quickly remind myself that sex is here to stay and start up the car. I move it out of the way before our new acquaintances decide to start their own towing and wrecking service.

They leave faster than we can spit a goodbye.

Chris and I pack things up and are hot on their tail. It's Tuesday and time is sinking. Only two days to go before my rendezvous with Annie.

We speed across the salt flats. The sun feels warm and I think Chris is the nicest psycho I've ever met. He studies the map and plans the shortest distance to Jersey. He wants to buy me lunch and by the time we roll into Salt Lake City it's noon. I talk him into Taco Bell. We pull into a drive-through, ordering a dozen cheese-and-bean burritos, two tostadas and four soft tacos to keep us company.

Who do we see in the parking lot? It's the two rest-stop dykes. They're out on the lawn having a tiff over lunch. The tall one is as thin as me. The other one is a sweet round-faced woman with long wavy hair. For a second we think they're going to punch it out. We give a friendly honk, but that doesn't get us far.

The rounder one gives us a dirty look. They drag themselves out of their argument, hop in their camper and pull into traffic.

"Oops, one of them forgot her hat." Chris spots a big black ten-gallon hat on the grass. We decide we'll just follow them down the interstate.

We race down the road, slurping burritos and dodging traffic. We're in Mormon country, telling Mormon jokes, and I feel like I've made a new best friend.

He's loaded with money, he finally tells me. He has a trust fund from his mother's mother. Why he travels this way is a mystery to me when he could fly anywhere he wants.

"I just ignore the money and live," he says when I ask.

We stop for gas and he's paying with a big bill. He's got a wad of cash an inch thick. We're on the highway again, with the sunroof down, and I let him drive. The sun blazes against our brows as we watch for signs to Cheyenne.

We look for the rest-stop dykes on the road. I notice a mean-looking, oil-burning Dodge Dart on our tail. The driver is a hard-nosed youth. He sits low in the seat and looks like a rodeo refugee. He wears an oversize black rustler hat similar to the custom-made ten-gallon number that belongs to the dykes. I put on the hat and give a look across the lane as he makes eye contact. He tips his hat and waves, motioning for us to pull off the road. We shrug our shoulders and keep moving on. The Dart stays close on our tail for two miles when we finally see the camper chugging ahead.

We speed up till we catch them. Chris slows to sixty miles per hour. I have on their hat and motion out the window, pointing as we pass alongside. While we're doing that, the Dodge passes us all and the driver tips his hat to me. I try to get the dyke's attention, but they're still arguing. When they see us they speed off like we're stalkers. The Dodge driver keeps pace at our side. He waves again, trying to get us to pull off the road. For the next few hours this whole scene goes on and on, in intermittent spurts, with us, the camper and the Dodge Dart, like a three-way orgy of hat-tipping madness on wheels.

Hours later the rest-stop dykes pull off to gas up at Cheyenne. They speed through town with us on their tail, the Dart on *our* tail. This is starting to look like one sick party. They pull to a stop at a Chevron next to the town hall. I can see that they're madder than shit with us.

The camper comes to a stop and the round, shorter woman hauls out of it in a full rage, screaming, "What the hell do you want from us? I'm goddamn going to the sheriff, you assholes. Leave us alone."

"I think they're having a really bad day," Chris understates.

I hold out her hat and say, "Hey, you left something behind in Salt Lake and we were just trying to give it back to you."

It felt so good to be right for a change. I was relishing the feeling. Suddenly the Dodge Dart comes driving up from behind. We all turn and look. The driver gets out and says, "Hey, you left something behind in Salt Lake," and he hands me a black hat.

"That's not my hat," I say.

"That's Sharon's hat," the round woman says.

"Oh, I thought this belonged to these guys. I found it at the end of the parking lot at Taco Bell."

The women take both the hats without a thank you. They hop in the camper and as an afterthought one of them says, "Next time just keep the hats, fellers." They drive off screaming at each other, still working out their highly dysfunctional relationship on the road.

6

The Redhead

"Nebraska, Iowa, Illinois and we're still not there? Shit! I'm never going to make it," I say out loud.

We skip the notion of sleep entirely and double up on our driving for as long as there is road. Exits to roadside U.S.A. whizz by us in a blur. Chris and I drive this poor Tercel through the much overrated heartland of America. If we were wanted criminals we'd be a hard catch because we aren't leaving an easy trail.

I take the Cornhusker State and he takes Iowa. We both split Illinois through the middle. When I'm driving he rests in the back like a baby. When he drives I agitate in the back like an old man, which I'm not, except in moments like this. Somewhere on the side of the blurry road I call Annie Sprinkle and tell her my progress. We agree we'll meet Friday and I'm relieved.

I curl up in the backseat. Before I know it another night and day has come and gone. Chris drives like a pilot, with a perfect command of the wheel. He says it's sexual to him. Driving cars, that is. Maybe he's got a point because I know what road vibration can do.

I ask the inevitable. "Do you ever have sex anymore? Can you?"

He shakes his head and says no. He spins off into an awkward moodiness that almost lasts another day. I don't blame him in the least.

We're cruising heartily into another evening, bumpy trail and all. I'm just counting my luck for keeping him on board. Nearly halfway across the country and not a single problem with the car.

About ten miles east of the Indiana border, when I'm half asleep, providence steps in to challenge my luck. We run over a huge tailpipe lying in the middle of the freeway. A mile later, as we hightail it across the flattened land-scape, we lose our muffler.

I'm up and ranting: "Shit! We're going to have to find a place to fix this thing."

Heading east on an access road next to the freeway, we slow to a snail's pace, looking for a garage. A man named Fred is running the only repair shop near the Illinois state line that's open for business after five o'clock. He just can't pass up a buck from hapless motorists like ourselves and stays open until midnight.

We backfire the entire way down the road. By the time we chug into Fred's garage, nasty fumes are seeping through the dash. We are really out in the sticks and totally at his mercy.

Outside, Fred waits in his coveralls, picking his teeth with a straw. Boats are parked on his lot along with a stack of old tires a mile high. He motions us through the garage, which with its two large doors looks like an old barn.

"Hope he isn't distant kin to some cowboys I met in Grants Pass," I say, remembering all too well my little dance with the firecrackers.

I jump out first, trip over a pile of discarded parts and send a hubcap spinning through the air and landing at Fred's feet. Fred bends over, splits the seam of his pants and tosses the hubcap like a Frisbee. It crashes near a sleeping dog.

Fred doesn't miss a beat and takes us inside, where a basketball game blares on the radio. When he bends over his potbellied stove, his bare ass peeks out through his ripped coveralls, but nothing is made of this. I am already calculating the damage, wondering who is supposed to pay for the muffler.

Chris says not to worry, he'll cover it for now.

Fred takes his time poking at a small fire burning in the stove and finally says, "Can't do much for ya until yer engine cools down.... How about a beer? It's warm, but it'll fill ya up."

We shake our heads, no.

On the wall is hanging a *Sports Illustrated* swimsuit centerfold. When Fred catches our gaze he starts bragging about his wife and how she gives it to him anytime he wants. Chris likes this, but I roll my eyes. I ask him what favors he does for her in return. Fred says he takes her hunting, and then offers to show us his rifles.

We decline.

We are hungry and have gone half the day without eating.

"Where can we get a bite to eat?" I ask.

"I suggest you head up the road to that truck stop you passed on the way in. They got an all-ya-can-eat for six-ninety-five. Ask for the redhead."

By now the sun is long gone. The truck stop is ringed by tractor-trailers and flashes a brilliant yellow GAS...EATS...BEER neon sign. Next door a motel offers

BEST REST...QUEENS IN ALL ROOMS. I very much doubt that.

The decor inside the diner is homey, with checker-board wallpaper, green cloverleaf carpet and wagon-wheel light fixtures. The buffet is fenced in like a corral.

Chris and I sit down in the nearest booth. I quickly surmise that our collective weight is at least two thirds lighter than that of any other individual patron. Our eyes bulge at the humongous plates of mashed potatoes, dev-iled eggs, macaroni and meatloaf dripping with gravy.

Across from us, two sisters, having just finished a bucket's worth of chicken, brood over their plates. No one in the entire place is speaking except the snappy waitress. She doesn't have red hair.

But *he* does.

Out from the swinging doors to the kitchen steps our freckled, six-foot redhead waiter carrying chocolate cake to the silent sisters. The sisters pounce on the cake before he sets it down. His nostrils flare and he slaps their check on the table.

The redhead spots us and his eyes light up. He saunters over to our booth and seems extra happy to see us. He leans forward and asks in a low insider's voice, "So what will it be tonight, gentlemen?"

"What do you recommend?" I ask Eric, assuming that is his name from the tag hanging on his shirt.

"I recommend you go eat somewhere else," he quips with sardonic glee. "Unless you have iron stomachs."

We like his wild laugh and it seems we have found a friend. We're ready to chow down and forget about the car for a while.

Eric is a good-looking boy no older than twenty-five. It is a busy night, and he's already making his coffee rounds, every so often throwing us a sidelong, sarcastic glance when yet another dessert is ordered by an over-stuffed eater. He is soon back at our table.

"So what's your hurry?" he says.

"Hurry?"

"You think I don't see you glancing at your watches? What'd you do, rob a bank?"

I was beginning to wish obnoxious young men like him would mind their own business. I say, "No, we're not in that big of a hurry. We're just waiting for the local redneck to finish working on our car."

"Well, there's plenty of them around these parts," he says.

"So what keeps you in a one-horse town like this?" I ask.

Eric levels his eyes at us and replies, "The love of a good strong man."

I throw a glance around the diner. "Does anyone know?"

Eric shrugs. As a family of six wanders in he says, "Why don't you try the lasagna before it disappears?"

After we've taken two helpings around the buffet, Eric rescues us with a cup of mint tea. He jokingly begs to be kidnapped.

"I've got to get out of this place. These people drive me crazy. I mean, sometimes I feel like I could go psycho here."

I spare him the details of just who he's talking to when it comes to extremes.

He makes a futile attempt to sell us dessert, but then advises against it. Chris tips him so well he nearly chokes us with a friendly hug before we get out of the place.

When we return to the garage, Fred is under the car,

cussing. He is wrestling with a new muffler and struggles to pull his butt off a ratchet. I get under there with him, and we're nose to nose as we study the muffler he's installed.

"You folks better keep an eye on your oil. And I don't know how much farther you plan to drive with this thing, but your shocks are almost gone."

I am praying he isn't going to explore this further, because the more he looks the more he'll find. I just want to hit the road.

"Where you headed, anyhow? I've seen a lot of you folks come through here lately."

I don't ask him what he means by "you folks," but I think I know. I look at Chris and feel like Grants Pass is about to start up all over again.

Ten minutes later Chris pays Fred for his services. We jump inside to start the engine, planning to make a quick exit.

"So did the redhead fix you up with something to eat?" he yells while we back out of the garage.

We nod yes, yearning to get the hell on the road.

Fred turns around to pick up his tools, and as an afterthought adds, "Yep, that redhead knows how to treat a person right." And then he says, "Yep, that red-head...he's my wife."

And off he walks as we turn east, our mouths hanging to the floor.

7

Bosom Ballet

Friday morning, nine o'clock, and after more than three thousand miles of road we approach Patterson bedraggled and bottom-sore. We feel like a runaway train loaded with amphetamines, but the only thing keeping us awake is AM talk radio. We find our first shock jock of the East coast crucifying gays for the upcoming march on Washington.

In a sudden verbal blast I learn that Chris is what I dared not suspect from the start: a potential bisexual. I'm riveted to his comments when he lashes out at the deejay. His quiet mood is suddenly broken on our approach to journey's end. He gets lost in a rant, almost yelling at the radio. And then to top it all off, he admits he fantasized of sex with me somewhere between Ohio and Pennsylvania. I want to scream. Either for joy or fear, I'm not sure which. It seems that the encounter at the garage and the truck stop with the two lovers had got him thinking.

I can't imagine what he wants from me and bite my tongue to keep from asking the obvious. *What did you have in mind?*

So, we're limping along with this new revelation.

Limping, because Cleveland gave us our first flat from a
pile of broken glass outside another truck stop. We're still
riding on the bald spare.

By the time we pull into Patterson, I'm so tired I see
double. Chris is sweating pearls. He's not happy to be
leaving my company. I feel an attachment has formed.

We hit town in the morning rush-hour traffic and
can already feel the beat of the Big Apple pulsing in our
groins. We exit the freeway at the spot where we plan to
meet the owner of the Tercel. We're soon sitting on the
curb, waiting for him to come. Chris is looking as sad as a
man can look.

"So where to? You really going to go to Maine? You
think it's going to be good for you to see Claudia?" I'm
asking.

"I don't know what the point is. What do you think I
should do?"

I feel freedom licking at my feet and wish he could
feel the same. Only four days since we met and the West
has faded far behind. I barely know this man and don't
know what to say. I point to a matchbook cover on the
asphalt. It says "Learn to be a Psychic," and we both laugh
for no reason.

"Come on with me to New York. We'll take the bus in
together. You can get a train from Penn Station for New
England, if that's what you need to do."

The owner arrives in a wrinkled suit and scuffed shoes
and is one sleazy dude. His hair looks like he's greased it for
seven years with chicken fat and left in the bones. He's
smelling like the flat wasteland surrounding us. And he
doesn't give a shit about the bald spare. We're paid in crisp
twenties for the muffler and he says to keep the change.

We grab an express bus into the city. The sad-looking

landscape, blighted by industry, whizzes by us as Chris asks, "Do you think I'll make it?"

Crossing the George Washington Bridge, I'm listening to his heart and for the first time I think I see fear in his eyes. I don't know why he's going back to Maine.

I grab at a cliché and shrug, "Sure, you'll make it, if you want to."

The towers of Manhattan loom to the south of the bridge. The cool morning sky is streaked with brown ugliness that hangs like airborne slime. I scribble down a number for Chris, a way to leave me a message, and tell him to give a call.

"Maybe I'll come to Maine after the march on D.C.," I say, not knowing why I say it.

"Sure, whatever. Maybe we'll cross paths again."

I wonder why I don't just let this one go. I doubt myself in the worst sort of way. Why the hell am I such a magnet for guys like him, living out on the edge?

We exit the bus at the Port Authority. The streets of New York hit us in the face five times over with backhanded slaps. When you've been on the open road cruising the wide, forever landscape, and suddenly you're standing on the streets with the stinking trash blowing in your face, amid pimps, hustlers, con men, tourists, rising decibels and a disappearing sense of time, you know for a certainty that the heartland is a pipe dream and the West a pony show. Here's where truth and desperation begin.

We hop in a cab for Penn Station. I wonder why I'm taking this man to his train. He's retreating into a shell of silence and says, "Would you come up to Maine...please?"

I say, "You're a masochist if you want me for a friend."

And he says, "Stay away from knives!" His smile is maniacal.

When he grabs the train for Boston, I'm glad we've said goodbye.

I walk to Annie's carrying my one small bag. I feel like a shower would wake me up and wash Chris out of my mind. I stroll through canyons of high rises. I buy a hit of ginseng at a Korean market before the lunch rush begins.

It's Friday in Manhattan. The weekend has begun long before the end of the day. I walk the final seven blocks up Lexington through Little India and ring the bell of Annie Sprinkle, Queen of Tantra and diva of the postporn scene.

"Hi. Come on up," a kitten voice, smooth as velvet, purrs over the intercom.

I push on the door and stumble in. I can smell her incense eleven floors down. It's like returning to an ashram. Everything in Annie's world speaks of the sensual. I am gliding on air up the elevator. The relief of leaving the streets soothes me like a satin slipper.

Annie opens the door to her Shangri-la. A mountain of clothes spreads out across the floor of her studio. The walls have changed since I was last here. The Goddess has invaded more than ever.

"Hello, Michael." She gives me a warm body squeeze, crushing me with her million-dollar breasts, and says, "Oh, you look good—did you gain some weight? Do you want some tea?"

She speaks with the lilting tones of a bird, her voice in melodious contrast to the gray of the day. Annie is always the perfect host and I'm soon sitting down under a purple canopy on her bed.

The room is like a temple, with images of goddesses and earth, soft and sensual. She's preparing tea and is in an obvious hurry.

"You know, we really do have to get going soon. I'm doing a benefit tonight in D.C. And I don't know what to wear yet."

She surveys her choices. I am relieved to see her after my long ride with Chris. Annie's my Leo pal and we cash in our Leo love secrets every time we see each other.

"Are you excited about the march?" she asks seductively. "I think it's going to be, um, sexsational. I can't wait to see all those dykes. What do you think I should take? Do you think I'll need all of this?"

I look over the dozens of petticoats, slips, heels, bras, pairs of pantyhose, wigs and enough makeup to do an army of drag queens, transgendered or otherwise.

With my assistance we pick out the look. She's quickly going over her list while packing, serving tea, feeding her cat and brushing her teeth.

"So, are you okay about coming back on Sunday? I can't stay longer than that because I have to start working on a film. We're doing one on orgasm!" She squints her eyes and giggles the unmistakable Annie giggle that has won my heart for years.

Annie Sprinkle, the postporn modernist, has tickled and challenged the sexual taboos of the radical hip for a decade. Annie Sprinkle, the film star and former sex worker, has made a life mission of sexuality. Annie Sprinkle, the lover of men and women alike, the oversexed goddess who celebrates her slutness finally announces after an hour of packing, primping and phoning that she is now ready to leave.

No sooner have I dragged the luggage down to the street than she has tipped her doorman, collected her mail, left a key for a friend and hailed us a cab. Annie moves fast. We ride to a car-rental agency. She's reserved us a baby-blue sedan with enough room for a queen, or two, or three.

"Will you drive, Michael? I mean, I would be *soooo* honored if you drove. It would give me time to prepare for the benefit."

I do her the honor despite my bloodshot eyes and twisted sense of time, despite three thousand miles of road under my feet. We pick up two other friends, Denise and Carl, for the long ride ahead. With the Queen of Tantra we drive out of Manhattan, headed down the eastern corridor for D.C.

Annie lights a cone of incense in the sedan and asks, "Do you think all these cars are going to the march?"

Thousands of vehicles barrel across the Verrazano Bridge. Every car is packed to the core full of seeming queers.

"Look, a car full of dykes. Oh, I'm so excited." Annie waves, flashing her pearly smile.

Bumper stickers shout loud and clear that queers have overtaken the highways.

"Wow, look at them!" Annie points at two dykes on the hump of a Harley, gunning down the road. Annie smiles at everyone and everyone smiles back.

By the time we hit the turnpike we're but the eye of the storm. Hundreds of cars, vans, buses and motorbikes are headed toward the march. We enter our first tollbooth and excitement rolls across the lanes. Catcalls, whoops and screams are traded as free as wind. And this is just the start.

"God. This is *soooo* sexual. I never knew the turnpike could be such a turn-on. I feel like all these cars and people are just a big orgasmic sexual orgy of traffic."

"Hey, Annie—truckers have known that for years!"

"Hee-hee. Oh, God, this is hot!" Annie fans herself in mock excitement.

There's more honking, yelling and screaming across the lanes. By the time we've gone ten miles Annie has stuck out her feet. She does a foot dance for the erotic pleasure of our fellow travelers. With each new on-ramp traffic slows to a crawl as hundreds of cars wait to get on the freeway. This gives ample time for a growing party on wheels. And each time we all slow down for the next on-ramp life gets livelier and a bit wilder.

"Dykes and fags. I love it. We're taking over the world," I yell.

A car full of lipstick lesbians pulls alongside. They roll down their windows and start yelling at Annie, "Bosom Ballet, Bosom Ballet."

Annie blushes. She kisses the window, bright and pink, seductively licking the crack of the window.

Cars are packing around us, waiting. Annie finally pulls out her tits and pushes them out the top of the window. Horns are sounding and people are screaming with delight.

"I think we're going to start a riot," she says.

We turn on the music and crank it up loud. Annie slips on two white evening gloves and begins her Bosom Ballet. Engines are roaring and carloads of dykes are going ballistic. She jostles her breasts to the beat, swinging round and round, side to side, up and down. One breast to the top, another doing circles, both meeting at the crack of the window, pairing off for a twisting descent and then more.

A bear of a man pulls down his pants and flashes his cock out the door of a van. Another carload of dykes unleash their tops to the music as we all continue crawling through the traffic. It starts a trend, and blouses and bras pop open by the dozens. Liberated breasts become a new freeway style.

By the time we approach Delaware, the highway is a riot of performance art on wheels. Tantric madness has settled in. Cars are swapping lanes and horns are blaring loud. Everyone is cheering for Annie, Queen of Tantra, Queen of the Turnpike, Queen of the Queers. Her first one-woman, postporn, turnpike exhibition is a rousing success and the mood is infectious.

"I never did it with the turnpike," she coyly declares.

And I silently wonder if the New Jersey Turnpike will ever be the same.

8

Down the Tantric Trail

"**I** just love sex. I just love the freedom of having sex anytime you feel like it. You can have sex with nature, sex with people, sex with buildings, sex with freeways...all you have to do is open your eyes. The world's a very sexual place."

Annie is finally sitting back and enjoying the ride while poor little Delaware slips by in two short blinks of the eye. Incense is burning from the ashtray and a red-as-blood rose sits on the dash. A satin scarf is draped over the seat and our tantric ashram on wheels seems to float effortlessly down the *sexational* road. Wherever Annie travels, the goddess seems to follow.

"What's the best sex you've ever had?" I finally ask, knowing this will keep us talking for hours.

"Oh, that's a hard one," she says thoughtfully. "There's so much sex to choose from. Maybe the best sex I've ever had was with the sky, that was the ultimate."

"The sky?"

"Yeah, I once had an affair with the sky for nearly a year. I was at this women's retreat center, learning how to talk to plants. Anyhow, I was on a break from everyone. I just laid out in the sun and started talking to the sky. The sky was suddenly communicating with me. I felt so connected and it became the most incredible sex. It went on forever.

"So after that I would carry on, anytime I wanted, with the sky. Once I was looking out a window and I was asking, 'Is this real?' All of a sudden a balloon popped up in front of my window, drifting toward the sky. I knew it was as real as I wanted it to be. I think the sky was my best lover ever."

I make a mental note to explore this sky thing further.

"But sex with nature is great. I have always thought of the earth as a lover. Just let me loose on a field of grass. I love to lick grass. To give a lawn cunnilingus. There's so much sexual energy in the earth. It's like you could light a whole city from connecting with the earth.

"And I love sex with waterfalls. Oh, my God! I can go totally ecstatic under a waterfall. I love getting totally submissive and letting the water dominate me. I can lie under water forever and just spread my legs. It's *soooo* intense. Most people don't allow the sexual energy to flow with them. You know, a bathtub and a faucet will do the same trick if you can't find a waterfall."

"When were you first seduced, Annie?" I ask with a grin.

"By a waterfall?"

"No, by a person!"

"Oh, well. The first time I ever had sex was when I was sixteen, in Panama City. I was living with my parents. I didn't like any of the boys my age. But I was walking down the street one day when I met this bearded hippy guy on a motorcycle. He owned this coffee shop in town and was a really cool guy, about ten years older then me. We started doing a lot of things together and we finally did the intercourse part. It was great. I didn't bleed like I thought I was going to. And it didn't hurt at all.

"But a month after losing my virginity I was so ready for sex that I would fuck anyone. It was like, 'This is the best thing in the world,' and I started sleeping with everyone. I kept a list of the first fifty guys I fucked. I was doing it with just one after the other. I think I still have that list somewhere.

"It only took a few months before I reached fifty. I had all combinations. Two guys, three guys, five guys at a time. I went absolutely wild. Nothing to really be proud of, considering some of the jerks I did it with. I started doing this in Panama City, then L.A. when we moved there. I absolutely loved fucking.

"The first time I ever did it with a woman was when I was in a porno movie called *Teenage Masseuse*. I was only nineteen, so I was still a teenager. I said, 'Okay, I'll try that, if that's what they want me to do.' I didn't get the hang of it for a while. It was really weird. Like there was nothing to suck on, or so I thought. Or nothing to stick in me, or so I thought. Women were so soft and mushy. I think I did it with three different women on that film. It was a one-day wonder. We had six sex scenes that we shot in one day.

"Now, of course, I love women. I'm such a lesbian. Which is why I can't wait to see all of those hot dykes at the march.

"But Michael, what about you? Have you ever had sex with nature...or a girl?" she mischievously asks.

We're nearing Baltimore and I think back to Idaho, years ago. Somehow the cool gray industrial skies of Baltimore seem the farthest thing from nature. But quite the appropriate place to talk about sexual encounters.

"Yeah, I guess I did nature once. But it was years ago, in southern Idaho."

"Really?" Annie has this way of leading people into stories, especially if they hint of eroticism or anything extreme.

"Yeah, but it also included sex with a woman. It was this really convoluted relationship I was in with the mother of my high school sweetheart. But nature somehow got involved."

"Really?" Annie's eyes were wider then ever. "You were with a woman?"

"I know, hard to believe, isn't it? But yes, I did it once."

Annie is laughing loudly.

"I had this girlfriend in high school, long before I was out. We'd been going together for six months but weren't having sex. We were just getting stoned a lot in her room. Her mom was this crazy artist who was instantly taken with me. Over time I was also in the mom's room smoking pot with her. Every time I'd come over to visit I'd be up with Cheryl the daughter, then I'd be down with Katherine the mother, and they were both deathly afraid that the other knew they were smoking pot with me. Anyhow, we were like one big dysfunctional family."

"Yeah?" Annie was riveted.

"A few years later I went to visit them in southern Idaho. The daughter had married and Katherine had divorced, but they were all living in this country farmhouse ten miles out of town. I was there for Thanksgiving. We'd finished eating and were polishing off a bottle of wine when Cheryl and her new husband Jeff went to bed. This left myself and Katherine in front of the fire. You can just guess what happened."

"What?" Annie's eyebrows arch in expectation.

"My ex-girlfriend's mother seduced me on the couch. It was right out of *The Graduate*. Anyhow, this led to the most clandestine relationship I'd ever had. Needless to say, I was invited to extend my stay and did so for two months. It was like a farcical comedy of musical beds. Each night I would bid good night and slip into the guest bedroom on the bottom floor. And then after everyone had retired, I would slip up the stairs into Katherine's bed, where we'd fuck like pigs. By sunrise I'd slip back downstairs before anyone rose.

"She was insatiable. Whatever discretion we strived for in the house, she abandoned it in public. Whenever the spirit moved her, she'd pull off the road. We'd be on the side of a country highway with both doors flung open, humping away.

"So one night at the farm we'd fallen asleep in her room after thoroughly riding the springs. She suddenly woke up screaming her bloody head off from a nightmare. It was horrible. She was hysterical, clawing at the sheets, thrashing around and spitting at the air.

"Well, Cheryl and Jeff came running in. I was sitting up in bed, nude of course, with my hands around Katherine trying to calm her down. They thought I was hurting her. Jeff slugged me to the floor. Cheryl held Katherine for dear life trying to calm her down.

"So there I was, naked, sprawled on the floor with Jeff straddling me in his boxers. Katherine was naked and sobbing in the arms of Cheryl. Suddenly the fifteen-year-old son, Jimmy, walks in and wants to know what the hell is going on.

"Well, it all came out in the open and was one hell of a mess. When Katherine became coherent she explained her gruesome nightmare. When Jeff demanded to know why I was in the room, Katherine finally shrugged and said, 'Okay darlings, we were fornicating hours before. All right? Now leave us alone!'

"For the next two weeks we just kept our heads up and continued to fuck."

"Oh, my God, Michael! That's the hottest thing I've heard in weeks. That is just *soooo* hot. But where did the sex with nature come in?"

"Oh, yeah. Katherine and I were always hunting for mushrooms out in the woods. Anyhow, I'd go for walks in the morning on the far side of the farm. Each morning I noticed this wildflower on the verge of blooming that was still growing despite the coming winter.

"On my walks I'd stop and look at it, admiring its vitality. After a few days of this it almost became like a friend. I'd look forward to seeing how it was doing. So one day, when I'm out there, I was sitting next to the flower and suddenly started to feel very sensual. I mean, it was just an energy thing, like you and the sky. Well, I guess the flower and I hit it off because the very next day it had bloomed this beautiful lavender blossom in the middle of the frost.

"I told Katherine about this and she thought I was absolutely crazy. That afternoon I took her out to see it. She immediately wanted to screw on the spot, which of course we did. The next day the blossom died. And the next day after that I decided to leave."

"Oh Michael. That's the most beautiful story I've ever heard. That is *soooo* beautiful." Annie is almost in tears as we cruise through Maryland. "That's a love story if I've ever heard one."

"Which one? The mother or the flower?"

"Oh, I guess the flower. Everyone's done their girlfriend's mother, haven't they? But how many have been seduced by a flower?"

9

Annie Sprinkles on D.C.

By now the sun has set, leaving crimson streamers across the cloudy sky. We merge into the Beltway and follow a constant flow of traffic until we turn off and head for the core. As we move toward the center of town something takes hold of us. The nation's capital, for all its blight, has turned completely lavender for the night.

Traffic backs up for miles. Every street and every car is teeming with people. Banners, signs and placards hang from shops and cafes. By the time we hit Dupont Circle we collide head-on with the unmistakable presence of a nation of queers.

The Circle is rowdier than a square dance on the Texas plains. Bodies, big hair, muscles, men, girl jocks, faeries, fags and dykes jam the night. Traffic barely crawls and Annie squeals with delight at the sight of all those girls.

"Oh, I've never seen so many beautiful women," she breathlessly whispers. "I want them all!"

We head west toward a warehouse loft where the benefit is soon to begin. Denise is in the back, busily choreographing plans with Annie, while Carl loads film for photos.

"So, Annie, what are you going to be doing?" I'm curious.

"Oh, you'll see. I'm going to make an extremely patriotic and wet contribution to the evening!"

I make a note to look for a raincoat before the show begins.

Finally we arrive in an alley next to a crumbling warehouse that smells like art of the alternative kind. Before we can even park the sedan a crowd of friends comes running to great Annie at the curb.

"She's here, she's here!" they're yelling.

I feel like I've delivered a star.

Annie unloads her bags of costumes and props with the help of a dozen hands. She is hurriedly ushered through the line of waiting fans. Only twenty minutes to go. We've made it just in time.

Outside the doors hang the severest of queers, hustling for attention with bloody tattoos and metal clanging against their skin. Broken glass scatters along the street and a trail of light peeks from the door.

Inside it feels nasty in a refreshing sort of way. With large ceilings and cold floors, the place is a dive, damp, dark and full of mold. Queer art screams from the stage and video monitors are stacked to the rafters, waiting their cues. The air is charged with excitement and the aroma of pot fills the room. Not an unsmiling face can be found. Hundreds of people are pressing through the doors to see the irrepressible Queen of Tantra, Annie Sprinkle, perform.

I quietly move to the front and run into old friends, Adam and Tom. We wander off to the side under a bank of stage lights and settle in for the show. I finally feel three thousand miles, four sleepless nights, psychos and Taco Bells exiting my skull.

The performance begins to a rousing wave of applause. Poets, singers, radical dykes and drag queens on wheels overwhelm the stage. It's the queers' turn in the capital. Tonight's our night to cut the ribbons of time and start a new life.

Each performer delivers a political message, but we're all already converted. It's Annie we want. The Queen of the Night is in the wings. We're all waiting her turn.

Finally, at the stroke of eight, she appears.

Annie parades through the crowd under a roar of cheers from the overpacked house. Wearing red and pink, with the highest of heels, she gingerly climbs the stage. We watch every step. Nearly everyone stands and the cameras roll.

"Well, I just want to say what a pleasure it is to be here with so many beautiful women!" she yells.

"Now, in honor of the Lesbian/Gay/Bisexual March on Washington, and in honor of our nation's capital, tonight's installation is for a city of beautiful, beautiful monuments. And I want to dedicate my body to my personal favorite monument in town...the Dupont Circle Fountain."

We're on our toes, not knowing what will come next.

"And now I'll begin by transforming myself into a fountain."

The music begins. Annie parades across the stage in her favorite tutu, corset and heels as she begins giving birth to her newest creation with the help of Denise. The speakers blast a patriotic march. To the amazement of all, she effortlessly stands on her shoulders with her toes pointed and her legs spread wide apart. She continues to talk while upside down. And she is not wearing panties.

"There are many beautiful fountains in the world, but tonight the Dupont Circle Fountain is the center of the world. And what would a fountain be without birds?

These are my favorite birds because they won't make a mess."

Denise hangs bird mobiles off Annie's five-inch stilettos, letting them circle in the air.

"And on a night like tonight, what would be better than some sparkling light to see who you're with?"

Now dozens of sparklers are lit one by one. They're placed in her costume, heels, hair and hands, lighting the stage.

"And what makes a fountain complete but bubbles and bubbles and lots of bubbles."

Dozens of bystanders in the first row are now blowing bubbles by the bottleful onto the stage for the special fountain effect.

The crowd is buzzing. Our imaginations are going wild. And then, with the national anthem playing loudly, drums rolling, trumpets blaring and all eyes upon her, the Queen of Tantra, the Bladder Girl of everyone's dreams, begins to let loose a five-minute golden shower into the air. It arches three feet high, creating rainbow prisms of light while splashing across the stage floor. Gallons and gallons of her spray fall in a circle around her. A fountain is born!

The house comes unglued as every soul in the room is rolling on the floor or screaming with utter delight.

On and on and on she pees, into the air with the sparklers, birds, bubbles and music. Never a more perfect replica of the Dupont Circle Fountain has the world ever seen.

Gallons later, and for those left standing, Denise carefully inserts a lubricated and brightly lit taper candle down where the water once flowed.

And in the hush of the room Annie finally invites us all to "Make a wish and blow," which we more than happily do.

10

The March on Washington

Bright and early on the morning of the Big Day I can't sleep in my hotel room. For one thing it's just a little too nice. Call me a white-trash queer from the wrong side of the tracks, but when I waltzed into the Sheraton hotel up to the fifth floor in an elevator full of attitude queens and their million-dollar luggage, and entered the most Republican room I'd ever seen, I just wanted to dirty it up a bit. I hate clean carpets.

Annie had left for the burbs with a pack of fawning friends and I took one of the only rooms left in town with Carl, the photographer.

So I walked into the room last night, put my little thirty-five-pound bag of clothes down on the bed and looked at myself in the gilded mirror. What I saw was a gnarly, stinking, dirty, bearded traveler with a few thousand rotten miles of dirt on his belly and egg yolk on his chin from a late night sunny-side up.

"My God, I'm so dirty I look like I have a tan."

I counted back the days since my last shower and made an early New Year's resolution to bathe more often when on the open road.

I took a shower and hit the bed. But sleep did not become my friend. I hate beds so stiff that you can't feel the floor touching your bones. No, I like beds that creak and moan and let you know the world's a jiggly place. I like peeling wallpaper and sheets that smell like cum. Doors that don't shut, faucets that leak and worn lime-green shag carpet full of cigarette burns. Then I feel at home.

I just lay in the bed all night long listening to people go off in their rooms and watching Carl breathe. Now that the sun is up I have a sinking feeling that this is going to be a testy day.

Right at dawn I walk out the door and snack on a few room service trays left in the hall from the night before. It's a feast if you don't mind picking through another person's meal. Plenty of cheese, shrimp and hard-boiled eggs, pieces of cake, custards, pie and unopened mints. There's even a whole crab and French bread under door 554.

I sit on the floor, pick over the crab, and wonder what they would do with all this leftover food if I hadn't come by. I feel like feeding some hungry homeless people. So I pick up a tray and pile on the food until I have a five-course meal of the best hotel grub one can buy.

While I pick through a fruit bowl beneath door 592 I hear two voices that sound very familiar. I strain to listen through the crack under the door for a while. They speak loud and hard. I wonder what sort of people are arguing this early in the morning. I try not to keep listening but then again, I want to know who they are. And I don't give a damn if they find me at their door.

"What did you do with the money? I saw you put it on the table last night, it was all there," says an accusing voice with a rasping curdle of a cough.

"Money, money, money, money, money. Can't we go anywhere without bringing your money misery along?" This voice is sharp and nasty and has a decidedly cutting edge for such an early hour.

"Last night we had eighty dollars before dinner. Now there's only a twenty on the table," says the first voice.

"How would I know what happened to it?"

Where do I know these voices from? I can't quite place them, but their argument hits a chord. It's Domestic Dispute 101.

"Now what are we going to do, Sharon? We're going to have to get through the whole day with only a twenty!"

"Oh, go to sleep, Trudi, or I'm leaving."

Now I know their names, and despite myself I can't tear away. I sit on the hall floor eating fruit, trying not to take sides.

"You're not going anywhere until you tell me what you did with the money."

"That's enough. I'm out of here. You can stuff this twenty right where it belongs. Up your ass."

"Where are you going?"

The woman named Sharon is stomping toward the door. I don't give a flying Jesus that I'm here on the floor. The door suddenly jerks open with Sharon hot on the run. Without blinking she steps right over me. My mouth is full of grapes. I choke and let out a gasp—if it isn't my two hat-chasing dyke friends from the road to Cheyenne here on the same floor as me!

I'm not surprised that our paths have crossed again.

Sharon is already down at the elevator. Trudi remains at the door. But then she notices me. She does a small double take, looking down as if I have appeared from another world. Her eyes turn big and red. She pulls her face back in growing shock. I sit cross-legged in my cut-offs, holding a bunch of grapes and hoarding a big pile of food on my tray. She clenches her teeth, shakes her head and says, "What the hell are you doing here?"

I shrug my shoulders and offer her a grape.

She's aghast. The elevator door opens and Sharon is getting in. Trudi stands there in an extra long T-shirt, barefoot and with no panties on as far as I can tell. She bolts right over me, squashing some of the grapes between her big and juicy toes. She runs down the hall and damn if she doesn't catch the elevator door just in time. The door springs open and they stand there a second. Then Sharon bolts out the elevator and runs for the stairs.

I decide to follow.

I pick myself up and gather my tray of food. Then I scurry to the elevator, hop in and ride down to the ground floor.

The lobby is as quiet as a tomb. There is no sign of my friends.

Out the sliding doors with my tray of food, on the bare concrete of the driveway, I prepare to cross the street when I feel them coming from behind.

Sharon is sprinting. She's got long legs like me and is putting them to good use. Off she goes, with Trudi not far behind. I admire their passion, as warped as it is.

I lose sight of them as I balance the tray on my shoulder and consider which way to turn. I walk but a few cool blocks and there they are on the Mall, in full form, fighting on the lawn. It's a shade away from becoming a full knock-down, drag-out brawl. It seems they might need a referee.

I gather my courage and walk over to them while they're still yelling about the money.

I swing my tray off my shoulder and say, "Listen, man, you don't have to fight. You all have been fighting like this since Salt Lake City. Don't you ever have anything nice to say to each other?"

Trudi doesn't like me one bit and says, "Stay out of this before I call the cops. There's a law against stalkers."

Well, she said the magic word, all right. I bow out and wish them a good day. I walk across the lawn and feel like such a fool, walking barefoot, and hoisting a tray of leftovers on my shoulder. I just want to disappear completely from the face of the earth for even bothering.

There I notice a level row of porta potties that are nice and clean. They look like a good place to hide. For all of the times I'd used one over the past twenty years I'd never been inside one when it's still fresh. I walk over and set my tray down at the end of a row and step on in.

Well, porta potties aren't all that bad when you're the first one in. They still have nice clean seats and no puddles on the floor. There's plenty of toilet paper and the blue-green fiberglass walls let in the nicest glow. It really is sort of fresh, cozy and well designed. I feel like I could spend a while in here, so I do.

I reach out and grab some food from my tray, then close the door. I have a seat and savor a nice slice of honeydew melon with a piece of sharp cheddar cheese. It's all so perfect. Just me and my porta potty on the Washington Mall.

I stay in my porta potty reverie, munching on my melon and listening to the birds. Then someone comes into the next porta potty and breaks the spell. Five thousand virgin stalls and they *would* have to get the one right next to me.

I sit quietly and listen. I hear a zipper go down and

pants drop to the floor. I hear the creak of the seat. Whoever it is has settled in as quietly as me. I can hear them breathing. They probably hear me breathing, too. Either they're piss shy or they're waiting for me to leave before they start cutting loose.

We both sit there, very, very still for a long time. It's a standoff of sorts to see who'll go first. But I have the upper hand. I don't have to go.

How many times have I been in that fix? Walking into a stall occupied on both sides in a quiet-as-a-mouse restroom, just waiting for a toilet to flush or water to flow to cover up the sounds I'm afraid I'll make.

Finally I hear something going on.

They zip up, preparing to leave, and I never heard them do a thing. So I stand up and open my door just to see who it is.

"What's wrong, couldn't get a B.M.?" I dare myself to say but don't.

The person is a big, tall, black woman wearing a denim vest with rabbit fur inside. Her hair is knotted in twists and ties. She carries a small bag full of deflated pink balloons and cracks a big smile even if it was a fruitless visit to the porta potty on the Mall.

I pick up my tray and follow. We're almost walking together for a while, heading for the Lincoln Memorial. We cross the grass, the dew soaking my feet. Towers of loudspeakers are being erected for the rally at the end of the march. And now the sun is fully up. I see where the events will soon unfold. Clusters of people are out walking around. A towering stage stands like a monument at the far end of the glistening lawn.

For all the beauty and glory of this morning, I feel like it's shaping up to be a very silly day.

Soon my porta potty friend is joining another woman and we're all walking together. I feel like introducing myself but feel shy. The two women start to talk. I pray they're not going to argue.

They don't. They seem to like each other without saying so. They talk about the breakfast they're going to have, with waffles and whipped cream. My porta potty friend says that she's going to smother hers with strawberries, syrup and slivered almonds on the side.

I love waffles. It sounds so good I almost follow. But I can see the shadow of old Abe Lincoln. I'm aching to give away my food, so I peel off at the reflecting pool.

Near the Vietnam Memorial I come across my first homeless persons of the day. Three men are camped out near the wall with their bags unrolled and their faces turned toward the sun. They are passing a cigarette from hand to hand and are working on a quart of Colt 45. They see me approaching with my tray of food. I feel like the good Samaritan of the day. I can finally see it coming, my big moment of feeding the masses, of stealing from the rich and giving to the poor.

I slowly turn toward the men fifty yards away and hoist my tray up, high and proud. My stride lengthens. Beams of sunlight fly off my face as I confidently approach the men with the best intentions in the whole world.

"Hey man, you guys hungry?" I take the tray off my shoulder and pull off cloth napkins that are covering the food.

They look at me for the longest time without saying a word. My smile is big and bright. My eagerness to feed overtakes my concern for whether they want it or not. One of them finally picks through the food with his scruffy hand. I realize I forgot to bring silverware or plates. His hand looks like it's been digging through trash bins for the last twenty years. His stubby fingers touch and discard each morsel of food as if examining slag. My smile, however intact, begins to fade. Their enthusiasm is not forthcoming. In fact, the more I think about it, the more disgusted I become. What got me to think I should take leftover morsels of food and pawn them off as charity?

Finally one of them takes a raisin scone in his dirty hand and crumbles it on the lawn.

"Looks like Sheraton to me," he says.

The other two agree. Then they ask me for spare change while letting me know in no uncertain terms that Sheraton food sucks. They aren't hungry, anyhow.

I gracefully tear myself away from this rejection and don't know what to do with my tray of food. It seems like a terrible mistake to impersonate a saint. But I carry on. I soon turn toward the south and offer it to a cluster of skaters on the steps. But they're up from last night, still full of drugs, and my tray looks suspicious to them. I then try to hock it off to a group of joggers at an espresso cart. They condemn me with their yuppie eyes. I just walk away.

I finally climb up to old Abe. When I get to the top of the steps I stand there awhile. A janitor is sweeping Lincoln's lap and he's doing a nice job. He slowly pushes a broom across Abe's long legs, knocking dirt to the marble floor. I watch the janitor at his task. He's an interesting-looking man, though so old he can barely hold the broom.

I take my tray of food over to Lincoln and just leave it at his feet. I say, "Want something to eat?"

The old man looks down. He gives me the biggest smile I've ever seen. His face is wet with sweat. He's mopping his brow with an old red hanky from the back pocket of his worn wool trousers. A pair of brown suspenders holds them up. He winks at me and says, "You just leave it there. I'm sure the birds would love a good meal," and keeps sweeping.

Birds? I'm somewhat dejected. Even Mother Teresa doesn't waste her time feeding birds trays of Sheraton food. The old man is right. Soon a flock of pigeons is down on the tray in a feeding frenzy that could last for an hour.

I wonder what Lincoln would think if he were alive today: an old black man sweeping dirt off his lap with a million homosexuals in town.

At ten o'clock I return to my room. Trudi and Sharon are back in 592, loud as ever. I begin to wonder if they ever get along. I tape a small flower on their door to brighten their day.

In my room I soak my bare feet, dirty from the streets, and give myself my weekly shave. My whiskers grow so fast that I'm always sporting this dogged beard. I want my face nice and clean. If there's going to be a million queers in town, I'm betting heavily that I'll find a way to belong.

Belonging has never come easy for me. The most compelling reason why I've come to the march is to see how I fit in. But with my unsettled ways, long days between showers, no credit cards, no closet full of clothes or circle of friends, I barely believe there's a place for me here.

By the time I'm out of my room and into the lobby the hotel is teeming with homos. And confusion immediately settles in. Everyone is dressed Calvin Klein perfect. Of course, what would you expect from a Sheraton crowd?

I wander out toward the start of the march. Contingents line the streets for blocks. Groups advertise their cause. But what cause do I belong to?

I feel out of place joining ranks with a state. Besides, which state would it be? Arkansas is sweet, but the state of my birth hardly gives me reason to walk in pride. California, Oregon, Maine. New York, Washington, Tennessee. I've lived in all of these, but none of them means a thing to me. Just places on a map, their memories long faded.

The radical faeries are bright and their colors attract. But when have I ever danced nude under the moon, or paid homage to the earth along with a hundred other men?

I like the platoons in the military crowd. But who am I kidding? I dodged the draft and think the military sucks.

I slowly walk around, looking for a group, yet none seems to speak to me. If there was a flag for Lonely Gay Drifters Who Live on Wheels, I might have jumped right in.

Well, I always did like a parade—marching bands, pom-pom girls, flag twirlers and all. The thrill of the drum major marching with his baton, tall hat, flashy tails and powder-white shoes.

But this isn't a parade. This is a march. A million marching, yelling, screaming people traipsing down the street in a fit of joy. A million women with women and men with men, holding hands, waving flags and bursting with pride.

Yet it really isn't a march, either, when I think about it. It's not precision teams, tightly spaced and keeping to a cadence. It's not armies marching to the sea. It is more a mutation of a parade, a variation on a march. And the noise is deafening.

People start to move and I unconsciously shuffle along. For an hour I'm in the middle of the street with the sun on my back and the breeze against my hairless head. I close my eyes and drift along in the stream of people like a sailboard surfing the sea. I take my chances and blindly merge with a group.

When I feel the brush of a man's hairy arm on my leg, I open my eyes. Much to my surprise, I'm marching in a wheelchair contingent of disabled gay men. And for some reason it all seems so very right, though I don't know why.

Now *here* is a group that lives on the edge. They know the curse of difference and loneliness for sure. And they're more mobile than me in their one-seat hot rods, cruising down the street.

The farther I walk, the denser it gets until Pennsylvania Avenue is a solid wave of bodies as far as you can see. And the bigger the crowd, the more I want to shout because I'm finally starting to feel like I'm fitting in.

I shuffle in with the group of wheelchairs, many of them electric. They're whirling through the packs of marchers ahead. I'm feeling more and more elated. For all my silly struggles I couldn't have found a more dauntless group. Sort of like bikers, but without as much beer, they ride their wheelchairs like Harleys. They're rough, tough-looking and full of reasons to complain, yet they proudly roll down the street to the cheering crowds.

Hours go by in the heat of the afternoon. I stay with the wheelchair group. I feel frivolous, full of pride and almost embarrassed to be on my feet. By the time we reach the White House I've made a dozen new mobile friends. For without a doubt these are the happiest Gay Drifters Who Live on Wheels I've ever met. I want to take them, wheels and all, to live on the road with me.

As silly of a day as I've had, I am caught in memories of my long road to coming out. Once I was but a drifting mess of confusion, hoping for someone to show me the way. I think of that someone who years ago appeared in the pink, lonely deserts of North Africa, on the back of a truck under the sweltering sun. That's where I learned I loved men.

But today I learned to love me.

PART TWO

11

The Marrakech Express, 1971

The hot shores of Morocco shone with a hellish glow across the choppy waters of the Strait of Gibraltar. Five hours crowded in the confines of a small room on a ferry from Barcelona were enough to send the best of men to the rails. I'd paid extra fare for a bed, entertaining visions of cushioned comfort on the overnight ride. I would have been better off in a seat. At least they were spread wide across the cabin, which had windows looking out on the sea. The beds were nothing more than small stinking hammocks, three tiers of them and fifteen to a room—no windows, no ventilation.

I had just climbed into a middle hammock when this giant of a man, smelling like a cigar, climbed into the top. His weight was so great that his torso sank to within six inches of me.

The ship tossed and turned. I learned firsthand what the sea can do to a healthy meal. By the time we got to the Moroccan shore I was puking off the side with half a dozen others and was never so glad to see solid ground. But the solid ground was not so glad to see me.

Customs wanted to know when my last cholera shot had been. I looked ever so much the street urchin, with stringy hair and a steel-wool beard. Without proof of a shot, I was rudely returned to the boat and sent back to Spain. So I suffered the ride back across the strait. This time I took a seat on the top deck, above the bridge, and watched the sun rise across the Mediterranean.

I was so fixed on finding my way to Africa that even this would not stop me. That afternoon I took a plane and invaded Morocco again.

This plan worked. Airport customs speedily welcomed me through with no queries about shots.

On the heels of six months in Europe, I was traveling with one bag and only fifty dollars to my name. I bounced out of the airport, hungry for adventure. The fabled tales of hashish, whores, exotic foods and men had not escaped me in my travels. Yet I had no idea that men, or rather a man, would become my destiny.

I took a bus to the center of town.

The marketplace in Casablanca was a sensory explosion of Arab merchandise. By the time I made it through the crooked streets and arrived at the train station, I was carrying an extra ten pounds of trinkets, useless save for the most important purchase of my trip, a wool djellaba.

I'd purchased a full-length black-and-gray striped robe with a hood. It was heavy and smelled like a barnyard.

In the bathroom at the train station I undressed under the watchful eyes of half a dozen men whose black mustaches hung low, like the wings of a crow. I put on my new identity. Despite my lily-white freckled skin and the fact that I was a head taller than any other man on the street, I was convinced that I now fit in. While I ran for the Marrakech Express a pack of chattering kids tugged at my robe, hawking everything from condoms to gum.

When I stepped onto the train I wasn't sure if I had boarded a livestock car or a passenger car—the floors had straw on them. Before going three feet I'd stomped through a pile of goat turds and discovered that my neighbors were a family of billy goats. They were all tied together with a long blue rope. This was held by the fragile hand of a woman so old that for a second I thought her part of the woodwork.

Amid children running up and down the aisle, I took my place on one of the wooden benches, which were a far cry from comfortable.

Finally the train lunged forward and off we rolled across the desert. Halfway through the day the train finally picked up enough speed to scatter dust along the tracks.

The Muslim women crouched in the far end of the car, concealed beneath veils. But the tribal women, Berbers no doubt, exposed their tattooed faces for all to see. Old men played card tricks on the floor. Young men pitched coins against the walls in a heated contest. The young men eyed me often with friendly smiles and a wink or two. At one point a young dark man with woolly brows walked by my seat. He suddenly flipped up the skirt of my robe to expose my bare legs. I was startled and didn't know how to respond. So I just smiled. They were laughing at me because I wore my djellaba without clothes underneath. This was far from customary.

Peddlers were crowding our car, adding to the melee. Children, old men and women made the rounds selling parcels of food, square meters of cloth, even hens. But the hash peddlers were the most intriguing. Another young

man came by with a kilo of it and a chillum for sale.
"Hashish, chillum" were his only English words. No one
seemed to mind. It was as common as selling popcorn at
the movies.

The train traveled through the night and no one
slept. The women clucked like their hens and the men
gargled their words. I didn't understand a word of this
language. But one thing I did understand. Not a man
there would take his eyes off me.

Early the next morning we entered the outskirts of
Marrakech. The train chugged by modern brown
buildings and dusty dirt streets. We finally came to a
nerve-shattering stop. In the distance I could see the old
city wall. We were outside the Medina in the new part of
town.

Out on the platform I rubbed my eyes. The towers of
the inner city rose against the distant Atlas Mountains and
an early-morning haze muted the brown clay walls of the
station. Carts rattled down the road, followed by leathered
men riding camels. Rows of taxis, buses and bikes waited
to find riders.

I stood there a moment, wondering what to do, until
I realized I was not alone. Standing on the platform were a
dozen more young tourists like me, scratching their heads
and looking puzzled.

A few of us banded together and took an old station
wagon taxi into town. The driver took one coin from each
of us. He then stuffed us in, baggage and all, including a
woman with a dog.

Our cabby was a short Arab man whose thin linen
slacks were spattered with coffee stains. He wore black
shoes with no socks. He also wore no underwear and was

hung like a horse. A French woman with hairy legs made note of that fact and we all laughed.

He took a circuitous route around town, and dropped us off at the gate to the old city. From there we separated. I made my way down the narrow corridors of ever-smaller streets. The buildings leaned inward, almost touching forty feet above. The sky was barely visible. Between open windows, over the street, hung bedding and clothes drying in the crisp morning air.

The streets were enchanting, filled with temperamental hawkers selling their wares. I was determined not to spend any more of my dwindling cash on unnecessary purchases—until I passed a stall selling long pieces of indigo fabric. This intrigued me. There were old men in the back cutting long swatches of cloth for resale. These were the foundations for turbans that sat on every man's head. I knew I had to have one of those to complete my indigenous look.

I haggled over the price, knocking it down a few dirhams until I thought I had a deal. They were amused that I planned to tie myself a turban. One soft-spoken man with the skin of a woman and fingers of a saint gingerly helped me into my first wrapping. He patiently settled a corner of the cloth on my head and began wrapping it in swift turns about my face. The turban built upon itself, forming a bird's nest that rose to a point.

They were all on the floor, laughing, holding their sides. I had been transformed into an Arabic conehead, which added another eight inches to my already imposing height. But I soon learned this was not a traditional turban in the least. No turban was worn to such ridiculous height except by tourists like me.

After the joke had worn thin I was shown the proper way to tie a turban.

I then walked down the street, fittingly attired in djellaba, turban and sandals. I stumbled upon a hotel whose hawker seductively drew me in. For a pittance I found a closet-sized room with open doors, shuttered windows and a small mat on the floor. The room was on the fourth floor, a height to which a few palms grew. A doorless opening faced in toward the courtyard and its tiled fountain. Having had two sleepless nights I fell fast asleep until early the next day.

In the morning I could hear birds twittering in the tops of the palms and the scurry of footsteps. The aroma of mint tea drifted up from below. Considering the mass commotion out on the streets, this was barely a disturbance. In the drafty room, sleeping under my robe, my bag for a pillow, I awoke startled by three young men who stood at my door, staring.

I jerked up, expecting them to be thieves. But they weren't. They just stood there, giggling in their light cotton robes, their skin brown and hair coal-black. Their eyes were warm and wet like a desert in a rainstorm. They held their gaze, watching me move and breathe. I wondered if I were that strange a sight. When I finally stood up, they ran away.

During the day I wandered around the Medina, sampling exotic foods. I sat in cellar cafes, drinking mint tea with enough sugar in it to sweeten the Nile. Hole-in-the-wall, back-door tea rooms, reeking of hashish and cigars, became my daily regimen. The saccharine Muzak of heavily orchestrated Arabic songs blasted over speakers.

The men of Marrakech were enticingly sweet or ornery and mean, depending on the time. It was a slow awakening, but over the next few days I began to notice that men were often staring at me. Not in fear, but with enticing gazes hinting of desire.

On the third morning I was once again awakened by the three staring faces. This time the oldest of the bunch spoke his first words. He asked me, in halting English, if I would come meet his family. I was much surprised to hear him speak. His words tumbled across his tongue like water rushing over stones.

At first I refused, but he pleaded. Soon I was following him through a back door, out of the courtyard and into an alley. The alley was almost a tunnel, the sky completely obscured. The darkness alerted me to the intimate danger of walking through Marrakech with a total stranger. My friend hurried us through the twisting, turning gloom of this hidden world. When we came to a door he sensed my hesitation.

Expecting a robbery, I held back. But he took my hand, pulling me forcefully through. Instead of more darkness, here was, unexpectedly, a busy street. The contrast in light was so severe that I covered my eyes with my hand.

Again we turned down steps, these ones leading to a small cafe. Old men squatted on the floor, sipping their tea and playing card games. It was a hash den. Their eyes rose not once from their game as my friend pulled me through a door into another dark alley.

I crept along in the blackness, holding his hand. He seemed excited and often turned back to look at me through ribbons of light that fell from above. His face was dark and his eyes twitched with an expectant glare. We finally reached another door, which took us into a narrow hallway. Here I again began to panic, wondering what he had in mind. The door behind us locked. At the end of the hall was another room filled with steam. He motioned for me to follow.

We entered a room with a large warm pool surrounded by ornate columns and tall, prickly palms. There was a big bearded man immersed in the water, his eyes closed. His robe and turban lay on the tiles. My friend turned and smiled. He came close to my face and looked at me steadily while pressing his thigh against mine. His tongue rested for a second on his lower lip, tasting the air, waiting for me to do something.

But I froze. This wasn't in the tourist guides. Something short-circuited in my head.

For a moment I thought we were going to kiss. I could feel his lips only inches away, the contours of his mouth nearly consuming mine. I watched his arteries swelling with blood and my head began to throb. His oval eyes, barn-board brown and deep as a cave, would not turn away. Sweat pearled across my brow and his fingers twitched.

My mouth opened, my eyes closed and I was about to lean forward when I realized I had foul breath. Where were breath mints when I needed them? I could smell his manly odors like the deep dark woods and suddenly, for no reason, old sitcom theme songs began playing in my head. The more intense it became, the more the songs took over my thoughts. He opened my eyes with his finger. But my mind became a montage of black and white kitsch.

Just when the theme song to *Gilligan's Island* came

through my brain, he grabbed me by the neck and pulled my face to his. Our lips quivered on an edge for a second too long. I could hear Gilligan yelling for the Skipper.

Suddenly I began to choke. I was filled with a laugh attack and pushed him away.

"What are we doing?" I chortled, gasping for breath. "I mean, I've never done this." I pulled away.

Baffled by me, he dropped his hand and asked, "Then do you want my sister?"

"Your sister!" I stammered. "Your sister?"

I shrugged my shoulders, totally confused. *His sister?* I shook my head, trying to get a handle on the sitcoms that played in my head.

He turned around, sulking, and led me to a labyrinth of stairs and hallways. It was a maze going deeper into the bowels of the building. The walls smelled like frankincense. Floors spun in delicious, hand-laid tiled patterns that were perfectly matched with the walls.

We finally reached the top of some stairs. He opened a heavy wooden door with intricately carved brass reliefs and handles made of iron. The door creaked open into a magnificent room piled with carpets and pillows. In the middle sat an aqua-blue, gilded pond full of delicate fish. Through high, grated windows open to the sun I saw long shafts of light striking a wall where a man sat humbly sipping his tea.

This wasn't his sister at all.

It was a man much older than I; he clasped his hands around the hot cup to warm his feeble body.

He looked up and grunted when we entered. My friend brought me over and whispered in the old man's ear. The man nodded and rang a bell. We were made to sit for a while at his feet.

Finally a houseboy entered carrying a small bundle. He silently walked across the room and handed this to the old man. They all stared at me while he slowly unrolled a cloth. There in his arms lay a carefully carved box with ivory inlay and a small, delicate latch. The houseboy produced a key to unlock it. Inside the box, on a small mound of smooth crimson silk, were dozens of stones set in rings of gold. There were a few small rubies, cut diamonds and semiprecious stones sparkling in the warm muted light of the room. He held them up for me to examine.

Everyone watched me, waiting.

Suddenly a light went off in my head, and I realized what was going on. I had entered a most exotic showroom, and this was nothing more than a sales pitch. The young man's job was to seduce me, lead me by the pants through the baths, and get me upstairs to spend some money on jewels.

When it seemed *he* wouldn't do, he had offered his sister instead.

I suddenly laughed at my revelation and grinned a toothy smile. I stood up, shaking my head. Disappointment grew in the room when I motioned with my hands that I had no money. They were not easily convinced and wanted to see my pockets.

I showed them my pockets. They were bare as the night, empty as a lake in a drought. And what money I had I kept hidden in my socks. The looks on their faces when they saw I was poor were a mixture of disgust and disbelief. The friendliness soon disappeared. The older man shooed me away with the tips of his fingers. The young man abruptly rose and motioned me to follow.

Now he was not so sweet. His hand no longer held mine. He took me to a door at the bottom of the stairs and then pushed me out into the street.

But not before I gave him a nice wet kiss on his cheeks. That's when I decided it was time to leave Marrakech.

12

Goats, Camels and Wormy Dates

Days later I found my way to Essaouira, a town bordered by an old Roman sea wall. Essaouira was a wannabe resort with its feet in two different worlds.

The first night there I stayed at the Rock and Roll Hotel. It was a swinging place owned by a French-Moroccan Rastafarian who blasted Motown in every room, rolled his hashish in papers and drank Asian beer. His girlfriend was Cuban.

Since the hotel really doubled as a noisy sex palace for a few local whores, sleep was a concept only. In the morning I stepped over puking patrons on my way down stairs and decided to explore the countryside.

Ten kilometers south of town, along a well-traveled path, stood a village on a small hill. A herd of goats overran the place—nothing escaped their hungry reach, whether shrubs, weeds, twigs or grass. They had mean dispositions, batting their eyes, snarling, bleating and snorting at anyone who dared to come within a few yards of them.

The village was camel-dung poor, with not more than three dozen houses scattered over the barren dirt. There were no streets, only footpaths between the buildings. The ratty well in the center of town was running low, its water copper-brown and smelling like rotten eggs.

I explored the town in a quick walk. One of the people living there was a Dutch artist who imagined himself to be Van Gogh. He had a a pencil-thin child who loved to eat dirt. They'd been there for more than two years. It cost them next to nothing to live there, and I wanted to stay—my dwindling American dollars could last me a week. The Dutchman said he knew where there were rooms for rent. He led me across a footpath to another house, passing unveiled women wearing hats, with pinned-up hair and henna-red faces.

In the center of a courtyard sat three men squatting over an open coal fire, roasting nuts. They were old and bent, and had no teeth to speak of. A witch of a woman in a doorway cackled at the shape of my turban and the crooked turn of my nose. Little did I know that the particular tie of my turban was worn only by bandits and thieves.

One of the old men stood up and took me across the courtyard to a small building. He offered me a room for only a few coins a week. I took it.

I set my bag down in my new white room. Obviously, hashish had a hand in its decor. White stucco had been poured over the dirt floor. Not a rock or a stick had been moved. In the center was a boulder large enough to be a stool, also covered in plaster. The walls, the floor and the ceiling all met like a sphere, with no hard edges anywhere. It felt like the inside of a pumpkin, although white, of course. There were no windows; over the door hung a threadbare curtain with the likeness of Porky Pig on it. How this came to be I didn't want to ask.

It worked. So I made myself at home.

It soon became clear that the whole village was a smokescreen for the hashish trade. Every day, young backpacking travelers like me would come to town looking for it. The old men would carefully wrap it up for them in newspaper, and another drug smuggler was born.

In the center of the village was one small store, called "the cave" because it was only five feet wide. Over the top hung a rusted Coca-Cola sign and a Pink Floyd poster decorated the back wall. The young Moroccan who ran it sold chocolate sodas, Mars Bars, burlap bags of couscous and hash. But no Coca-Cola.

The village idot lived with his dogs next to my building. They said he was crazy, and I didn't need convincing. He spent his days rocking on his heels, playing with his dong and looking like he was on a permanent high. His beard was so full of lice that a flock of birds could have had a feast on it. And when he foamed at the mouth, the flies gathered around him in clouds. Once a day the old woman who'd laughed at my turban took him a bowl of food. He put his face in the bowl, just like his dogs, and seemed happier than any of us.

Every morning almost the entire village rose at the same hour. We'd all wander out to this big field, squat, do our duty and use our hand to wipe up. No flush toilet, no toilet paper, no Handi-Wipes.

One morning, when everyone met for water at the well, we found that one of the poor peasants with us had stolen a crate of tangerines from the market in Essaouira.

It took me a bit, but I finally figured out that the whole village was full of disreputable types. Sort of like poor white trash, only Moroccan.

We were all standing by the well, picking through the crate, sucking on the sweet stolen tangerines, when three Swedes walked up. I had my head so far down in the crate I didn't hear the commotion at first. The locals were all chattering away while a man named Peter wandered into the village with two other companions, Joseph and Sylvia. The whole village stared at them as though the sun had just burst through on a cloudy day.

The women were cackling, which they always did. And the men stood up and rubbed their groins, which they always did at the sight of fair skin. The bratty village kids led by the pencil-thin son of the Dutchman ran in circles around the Swedes like fluttering moths.

The Swedes stopped at the center of town. The Dutchman was blasting Beethoven on a portable tape player. And were it not for the stench of the shitting fields, one might have thought the gates of heaven had opened up and cast three angels upon us.

Peter was a beautiful, fine specimen of manhood. He had blinding blond hair as white as fleece that fell in soft curls around his face. And his eyes were such a sea of blue I thought twilight was upon us.

Everyone watched.

He worked it, too. He wore a white woolen robe and sandals on his feet.

His skin was golden, not brown, not white, but golden. Just like someone took a pound of gold leaf and molded it to his face.

And what a body.

Even the old women were getting an eyeful of his chiseled arms and tanned flesh.

My heart pounded in my chest. My skin crawled across that desert floor until I was just one step away from pouncing on that fallen angel. No late-night, pipe-dream hallucination had ever produced such a vision as he.

Peter and his friends walked over to us and the box of tangerines. Joseph began talking in French to the villagers. That didn't get them far. They only spoke Arabic.

Frustrated, Joseph then tried a little Spanish but only met more blank stares. And finally, in English, he asked if there were any rooms available in town. Almost everyone in the village understood two English words: *"room"* and *"hashish."* And almost every young vagabond knew this was the village where both could be found in plentiful supply.

The whole town had a place to rent. Soon all thirty villagers were taking the Swedes by the arm and pulling in every which way to get them to come see a room. I pushed my landlord into the melee and the Swedes were soon walking with him over to our compound. Above my landlord's house was a long, narrow space with a dangerous stairway leading up to the roof. If you made it to the top you could see the ocean.

Peter and his friends took the room.

I made a welcome-wagon call within an hour, delivering a basket of tangerines and some hash. Unfortunately Peter didn't understand a word of English, but Joseph did. I learned they had come because they wanted to see Africa, just like me.

I left them alone to settle in.

That day, as on all days, I took my lonely walk to the beach. I imagined that Peter was probably a nerd and

Sylvia was probably his wife. Anything to downsize him to human scale.

After all, what was up with me and men anyhow? One kiss in Marrakech and now my whole world was spinning as to who I was. I prayed that sleeping dogs would lie, and then hit the waves. Much later, after swimming in the foamy surf I strolled along the beach, where I ran into Joseph and Peter frolicking and building a sculpture in the sand.

I was glad to see them again. From afar I watched them dancing around their creation. Then they saw me. They had the look of raccoons caught in the trash and tried to steer me away from the sculpture.

But that didn't work. Not with me, anyway. I poked my head around Joseph and saw a giant sandcast of a man. It had a two-foot phallus between its legs and purple seaweed that could pass for...

"Pubic hair?" I ventured.

They smiled sheepishly and I felt like a straight fool. They were giddy, giggling and carrying on. Now I was really confused.

Oh my God, they're gay and Sylvia's their...sister?

I must have looked shocked. I didn't know whether I was glad or mad. Was this a good sign or a bad sign? Were they lovers? It was all new to me! I ran away through the brush, passing a herd of albino camels chewing their cud.

Back in the village I stopped at the well and talked to the Dutchman for quite a while. His boy was downing tangerines while he picked at the paint under his nails. He said the whole village thought the Swedes were a sign from the gods. The old woman of a witch was predicting a flood of gold by the end of the day.

Fairie gold is what I thought.

When I returned to the courtyard, Peter was already back. He lay outside, sunning himself like a temptation of flesh with a sweaty long torso and Michelangelo legs.

He caught my eye but I fled to my room. Then he got up to follow. I watched as he stood at my door for the longest time without saying a word. That's all we did, look at each other.

Peter left me in the room untouched, but not before a few rivers of sweat drenched the floor. For hours I sat on the plastered rock in my room, looking out the door. I watched bearded men drift around in clouds of smoke and the village fool pull lice from his beard. I could hear the blond footsteps of Peter pacing in his room.

My inner world had shifted.

With a sigh I finally knew that this was why I had come to Morocco...to meet this man.

Days later, with tangerines filling my belly and my money in short supply, Joseph appeared at my door. He said they were about to travel south across the Sahara to the heart of Africa. I plunged into depression on my lumpy floor at the mere thought of bidding Peter such a speedy farewell.

But then Joseph said Peter had asked him to invite me along.

"He said what?" I stammered. My legs were shaking like Jell-O as I blurted, "Are you two together?"

He shrugged and said no. I wasn't sure if he understood what I meant. I wasn't sure if I understood what *I* meant. But I was satisfied with the answer and couldn't say yes fast enough. My bag was packed so quickly that half the dirt in the room came along with me.

So together we all hit the road. Sylvia, like me, was a new friend to them. She was as smitten by Peter as I. Her gaze was like butter, melting all over him. And if he were God, then I was the devil in her eyes because she didn't like the competition.

We stuck out our thumbs and went south into Morocco, hugging the sea. For days we traveled from one oasis to the next. We saw villages no bigger than a dozen goats and then lavish resorts like Agadir, with hotels and paved streets. The road at the end of the day took on a pink granite glow. Joseph and I called it the Pink Highway. Where it would take us, we were not sure.

Six days later we trooped into Goulimine, on the edge of the Sahara.

That night we all took a room in a hotel, which in fact was more like a stable. The first floor was covered with straw, full of camels and donkeys tied to posts with their tails swishing away flies. Their dung littered the floor and the old men were burning the stuff in a small fire.

Our room wasn't very private at all. It was just a big long hall on the second floor. There were big four-foot holes cut in the floor so the guests could watch their livestock and listen for thieves. We thought this sort of clever until Joseph rolled through the hole and found himself dazed among the goats.

In the dusty dawn an old man woke me up in a hurry by pissing in my face. He was aiming down below but had missed. I did not appreciate the shower. When I walked out to the market, I couldn't believe my eyes. Thousands of mean-spirited, sand-spitting camels with their big ugly teeth were being bartered and sold.

I woke up the others and we all wandered around the market. Despite the fact that this was the end of the road, there was a lot for sale. Beads, dyes, herbs and dried foods competed with radios, cassettes and electronics from Asia.

We walked through the market in our robes and turbans , but our pale faces and tall frames gave us away as impostors. Crowds would part for the Swedes.

At the far end of the market was a line of cargo trucks. Since there was no more road, we began bargaining for a ride south through the Sahara. The name of this game was contraband, plain and simple. Twenty trucks were parked with their backs facing the market, unloading their goods. Refrigerators, TVs, shoes, tires, bicycles, carpets, carved tables, ivory, rhino tusks...

Finally we stumbled across three leathery men who had a loaded truck tied down and ready to go. They were going south all the way to the border. We were jumping up and down because it looked like a ride. All they wanted was a few coins from each of us.

We agreed. Joseph and Sylvia ran around the market, buying provisions for the desert—dried fruit, nuts and dates. Back at the truck there were four more people in line. Two German women with their Turkish boyfriend and a peculiar Japanese man with a Clark Gable mustache and wire-rimmed glasses who wore a suit and a tie.

The Japanese fellow was carrying a suitcase, a shoulder bag and a case full of cameras, and he spoke the best pidgin English I have ever heard. His name was Henry.

The truck had a tarp and a million ropes holding down the cargo. First we threw our luggage up above, then climbed the side and carefully settled down on top of the tarp. The mysterious cargo towered an easy twelve feet above the ground so we were sitting several feet above the cab. The only way to hold on was to grab the ropes and pray.

The Japanese fellow was the last to ascend. He was

sniffing the air like a basset hound and asking the driver what was under the tarp. It was a sharp smell, with a slight putrid edge. We all noticed it, but then most of Morocco smelled that way. The tarp was full of dangerous, hard-as-rock lumps surrounded by soft mounds. Our three drivers only spoke Arabic, so nothing was explained.

The diesel engine was soon spitting fumes. We were bouncing across town, headed south for the great desert expanse before us.

That's when hell began.

We were twelve feet in the air, so every bump and turn sent the pile of cargo swaying back and forth, nearly heaving us off the truck. As we held on tight, the ropes cut and burned our hands.

We screamed to slow down, but the drivers didn't give a camel's shit. They took off at full speed across the desert floor. With nothing to shield us, the wind cut a hard path across the top, where we sat exposed to it and the sun. And furthermore, the cab was belching its foul-smelling exhaust in our faces.

Things couldn't be worse.

The Turkish boyfriend was an enterprising guy. He crawled toward the back to see if there was a way to get under the tarp and down with the cargo to stay out of the wind. He and Joseph struggled to peel away the tarp. They pulled it back a foot when they both arched over in complete disgust. Joseph looked whiter than normal and puked over the side.

We were riding on top of dead goats!

At least a hundred freshly killed carcasses were stacked in bleeding, stinking rows with their matted hair and nubby horns.

We were all horrified. Here we were riding on top a bunch of horns, heads, soft bellies and goat rumps all the way through the Sahara.

We were all screaming to stop. But our drivers continued their southerly trek for the desert.

By the approach of evening, not a one of us was spared. We were either windburned, sunburned, ropeburned, poisoned by diesel fumes or wretchedly sick from the smell of rotting flesh beneath us. We'd managed to shuffle a few carcasses around to form a small sunken pit in the middle with enough room for five.

The Japanese man sat at the very front, his feet planted on the cab, and holding the ropes like he was riding a wild and woolly camel. He sat there for miles, smiling maniacally and not speaking a word.

At nightfall, with surrounding dunes casting long shadows, we slowed. To our surprise we could hear the pounding surf of the Atlantic. This startled us all. From all appearances, we had been headed into the middle of the Sahara, but our drivers pulled to a stop overlooking a beach.

Three of us made a mad dash for the ocean. Peter, the Turkish boy and I stripped naked and took a dive in the cold surf to wash away the rotten day. We were bouncing on the waves and diving under the salty foam. The Turk had spotted a crab on a rock and was trying to catch it with a stick. Peter and I stood waist deep, the waves lapping against our bellies and the wind brightening our cheeks. His toes dug through the sand and pressed into mine. And I sucked in my heart a million miles deep and shook my head in the air.

Dinner that night should have never been eaten. The Moroccans built a small fire out of driftwood and the youngest put a big pot of seawater on to boil. The older man untied the tarp and hacked up a goat with a machete.

We stood back in horror as he dragged the thing off the truck and carved meat from its bones. The meat went into the boiling pot of brine. An onion was added, as were a few kilos of couscous. An oily gel that smelled like fat and a few hot-as-hell seasonings went in last. This became our meal.

It wasn't all that bad, or at least it was so spicy hot that we couldn't tell the difference. Afterward we drank sugary mint tea and stumbled off into the dark to make beds for the night, far away from the goats.

In the early morning the motley crew assembled at the truck for the second day of our journey. The feast of the night before had taken its toll. We all had the runs.

Our tormentors were rousing themselves from the cab, where they had slept. The older driver was as wicked as could be. He was a plump hirsute man with enough hair in his ears to form a hedge. He had the belly of a pig that bounced with each step, and we all joked that he was pregnant.

The young man was not a pretty sight, either. His face was full of misery. He had a large cut above his eye that oozed pus. He was clearly the underdog, since he jumped like a rabbit at the others' command. The third man was the only approachable one of the lot. He had a handsome face and a sense of humor. But he was also the cook, which was not a point in his favor.

After a quick breakfast of mint tea and bread we were narrowly ready for another ride.

That day the sun shined even brighter. By noon every one of us had puked over the side.

We were going far from the sea, and dunes towered

hundreds of feet high, like small mountains. The drivers seemed to drive by instinct. There were no signs of a trail, no ruts, no road, no markers, no footprints. They seemed to be following invisible highways in the sand.

The first stop of the day was well past noon. The youngest one jumped out, untied three large gas cans and poured diesel fuel into the tank. We all jumped off the truck to relieve ourselves, and things in that respect were pretty grim. Not one of us had a good stomach. Except for Henry. He seemed to be just fine. That is, until later that day.

In the afternoon we came off a bumpy trail down the side of hill. We were swaying back and forth, hanging on the sides, when Henry flew into a rage. He began pounding on the roof of the cab like he was putting out a fire.

He pounded and pounded, like a jackhammer, yelling at the top of his lungs. The driver stopped. Henry sprang up and gathered his things. The Moroccans were leaning their heads out of the cab, cursing like devil dogs. Henry leapt off the top and landed like a flying warrior on the desert ground. There he assembled his bags on his shoulders, picked up his suitcase and walked off into the searing desert.

We were in shock. Joseph yelled at him to come back. Henry shook his head, straightened his tie and kept on walking. We thought he'd never have a chance of surviving and pleaded for him to return.

But he was gone.

Finally the driver took off. We all screamed not to leave Henry, but they could care less. This fueled our conversations for the next few days, all of us wondering what became of poor Henry walking alone in the middle of the desert.

By the third day we wouldn't touch their food anymore. We lived on sugared walnuts and dates.

Swarms of flies followed the truck for miles. The three Moroccans just kept in their cab, out of it all, with us fools on top.

By the fourth day none of us were speaking. We just listlessly hung on the ropes, wrapped in turbans and scarves. Peter had grown so tired that we barely looked at each other anymore. We just gazed out across the landscape or followed the shadow of the truck as it crossed the dunes.

That night the whole lot of us huddled together in a pile as we slept. The Moroccans continued to sleep in the cab. Joseph swore the old man was buggering the boy under the steering wheel.

On the fifth day we came across our first tracks in the sand. Finally we were getting somewhere. The drivers seemed more than excited. In fact, we began to wonder if they had been lost all along, going in circles. Within a few hours we could make out a settlement on the horizon. On a flat and barren parcel of desert were dozens of buildings, so we thought. The closer we came, what had appeared as buildings turned out to be nothing more than cardboard shanties propped up against the wind, with a guard station and a roadblock at the far end.

We were at the Spanish Saharan border. Our truck ride had come to an end.

13

The Firing Squad

Thirteen trucks stood side by side. The border was just a strip of sand away. Almost as many trucks were on the other side, all with their tails facing us. There was no fence, no flag, no wall. Just a shantytown full of leathered faces peering out of cardboard boxes and wooden crates.

So this was the end of the road, Contraband City, where the real deals were made. A dozen men were waving their arms in the air. It wasn't exactly a homecoming committee, just a tribe of Berbers getting a rise out of seeing *girls*.

The Berbers were a shade more civil than our Moroccan drivers. A tall, elegant man wearing trousers and a turban was directing our truck in. When we finally came to a metal-crunching stop, we all jumped down so fast we left tread marks on the rails.

We unloaded our bags and kissed that stinking truck goodbye forever, without even a nod of thanks to our drivers, who were laughing like fools and spreading the news about the pack of idiots they'd found to pay them money for such a ride.

We walked toward the guard station and stood in a line. It did seem a bit absurd. There was no one in the station. And nothing but a small gate crossing to distinguish the border.

The Moroccans were freely walking back and forth, shifting cargo from truck to truck. Finally Joseph went to ask about the border.

The border only opened once a week, and tomorrow was the big day. That's why the smugglers were all there— to exchange contraband before the officials showed up. We were told that a military bus from El Aaiún brought a captain up for the weekly opening. Once he stamped our passports, we could catch a ride on the bus.

So we dug in for the evening right there on the sand. We watched them tear off the tarps and that wretched smell of rotting goats overtook the camp like a plague. The Berbers were all gagging, pulling scarves over their faces. Our Moroccan drivers were puking on the tires. All seven of us just stood there with our hands on our hips, nodding our heads saying one big, "Uh huh.

It was sweet revenge.

By evening all the trucks had exchanged cargoes and the Moroccans were back on their way. The Turk yelled, "See you in hell," and he had a point. If there was a hell they'd be there.

That night we partied. We were stone-happy drunk to be off that miserable rotten truck. The Germans dug out a bottle of wine, the Berbers brought over their hash and the Swedes pulled out tin cans of sardines while the Turk and I did a little soft-shoe on the desert floor. We had ourselves a virtual feast at the invisible border of Spanish

Sahara. And from time to time we wondered how ol' Henry was doing in his suit and tie in the middle of the dunes.

When the moon rose the two German girls went off to smooch across the border. Sylvia turned her nose up at them. She'd thought all along they were a couple of dykes and I did, too. The Turkish boyfriend just smiled and soon joined in on their fun. They were fucking by the guardhouse in the light of the moon and didn't give a shit what any of us thought.

The rest of us just fell asleep like exhausted soldiers after a forced march.

Bright and early in the morning we heard the roar of a bus barreling across the sand. Joseph was the first to jump up and see a cloud of dust as high as the sun. It was the military bus from El Aaiún.

We were all scrambling for our passports. None of us wanted to be left behind in this charming little place.

The bus came to a stop and half a dozen sloppy-looking soldiers climbed out. The captain stepped out toward the small shack of a guardhouse. He looked tough as nails. They opened the door, set up a table, and the square-faced captain seated himself in front of his papers, clicking his heels. We all snickered at the fact that those two Germans had been performing cunnilingus about eight hours earlier on that very spot.

The border was officially opened.

As the others lined up I trotted out to a field for my morning squat. The captain made a note of this.

Slowly each of us waddled through the guardhouse, rubbing sleep from our eyes, and waited for the stamp of approval before boarding the bus. Joseph went through and that only left Peter and me.

Peter stepped into the guardhouse. The captain wanted to see his passport and money.

He'd been asking this of everyone in line. If you didn't have a hundred dollars cash in your pocket, he wouldn't let you through. Neither Peter nor I had paid attention to this. When they asked Peter to show his money, he drew a blank. Joseph was carrying Peter's wallet in his pack.

The captain scowled when Peter yelled at Joseph to give him his wallet. He was a ruthless, play-by-the-book old fart. He refused to let Joseph give Peter his wallet. The guards stepped up and blocked Joseph. Peter argued till he was pink in the face trying to convince the captain to let Joseph give him the wallet.

But the captain didn't care. He said it was a trick and that if Peter didn't have the money on him then it wasn't his. The guards shoved Peter back and motioned me forward.

Now, I definitely did not have money—at best, ten dollars left to my name. I was trying to come up with something good to say on the money front. But the captain wasn't concerned about my money. He wanted to know why I was out there taking a long shit in the field. Then he asked to see proof of my cholera shots.

What the hell was it with cholera shots? For the second time I was refused entry across a border for lack of a shot.

The captain slammed his books shut and motioned to the guards to push us back to Morocco. Before we knew it, the bus had started.

We were left standing in Morocco with Joseph, Sylvia, the Germans and the Turk all looking on in horror. They screamed as the bus took off. It left us behind in a swirl of dust, but not before Joseph tossed Peter's wallet out the window. Joseph yelled from the bus that he'd wait for us in El Aaiún.

As the dust settled I turned to Peter and gestured to ask him what we ought to do. I felt like the fool because, come to think of it, Peter and I had never spoken a word to each other.

We turned in a big circle looking at where we were. No TVs. No radios. No cars. No crooked hawkers trying to steal our last coin. It *was* the end of the road.

But we were not alone. It just felt that way.

About thirty yards away a hairless old man with a set of wooden teeth peered out from his curtained door. Two wooden crates turned on their side were his home. Actually, they were his store.

He brought us over to his little hut, no bigger than a bread truck, and let us peer inside. He had all sorts of stuff in there, from AA batteries to canned pears. The shelves were jammed with overflow contraband from the trucks. He made it known that everything was for sale.

This was reassuring in an odd sort of way.

We walked outside and let out the biggest sigh. It looked like we had no choice—we were going to have to wait a week. There was no way in hell either of us was going to take another truck back through Morocco after what we'd undergone.

We took a cue and made ourselves a home out of an evacuated box. It was a nice box, made out of cardboard and high enough to squat in. There were two small broken toaster ovens inside to weigh it down from the wind. At four by eight feet, it had enough room for two men to sleep in.

That night Peter and I just quietly fell asleep in separate corners of the box. We didn't have anything to say because we couldn't talk.

I lay there for the longest time, staring at the roof of the box, listening to Peter sigh. He still looked ever so much like a god, only a depressed one. Then this *god* started to snore. Not just a sweet-little-baby snore but a dirty-old-hairy-man snore with phlegm in every ground-rattling breath.

I didn't get a wink of sleep.

The following morning my eyes were glued closed with a ton of grit, and I stretched my legs outside of our cardboard box. I stood up and crossed the desert floor like I was walking on a crunchy pie. The wind off the dunes blew sand up into the air, in my hair, up my nose and into my lungs. I sort of enjoyed breathing sand. It was better than stinking exhaust or rotting goats.

I went foraging for scrub brush to build a fire for tea. Then I saw Peter pop out of the box and run after me. He had a smile on his face and sailed in the wind with his turban fluttering behind. His golden skin and blue eyes mirrored the hills and sky before us. His mood had changed.

He yelped. I laughed. And off we sped in a chase up the dunes, over the crest toward the rising sun. We laughed—parched, guttural laughs that crackled through the earth. Peter was fast. He caught the corner of my robe, pulled me down, and met me eye to eye.

What a tease he could be.

Up he went again, running along the top of a mountain-sized dune. The sun kissed our faces as we raced along.

When we came to one crest, we stopped.

Across the valley we saw a band of men far away on a neighboring dune. At first we were startled.

The more we studied their silhouettes, the more we could see they were a military patrol. They rode two abreast on camels, their rifles hoisted in the air. They cast long shadows across the valley. We began waving. And then we ran. Ran like speeding bullets, ran with the wind, not away from but toward them.

Most people might have seen a band of gun-toting camel riders and hid behind a hill. But most people hadn't watched *Lawrence of Arabia* a million times.

We were electrified to see such a scene. Men in robes, turbans and gun belts, all riding behind a fluttering flag. Off we sped like two desert foxes into a snare.

By the time we hit the bottom of the dune, they had seen us. Suddenly, in full fury, they charged. Two shots rang past our ears as soon as our feet touched the valley floor. The riders thrust their heels into the camels' flanks, scattering dust and spit. We were alarmed. Those bullets seemed a little too real.

Within minutes we were encircled, rifles aimed at our heads. Very confused, I stood there grinning a stupid-looking grin.

Peter was the first to go down; a man took a swing with his boot and kicked him to the ground. Then I was hit on the back of the legs and fell too. They were yelling in Spanish in loud, angry voices. A soldier got down from his camel and pulled us up by the scruff of our necks.

They then tied our wrists behind our backs. Four men dismounted, jammed rifles into our ribs and shoved us forward.

Terrified, we didn't know what to do. They were

asking for our passports, which we'd left back in our cardboard box. We were in a sorry state.

For the next two hours we marched ten kilometers through the valley of dunes. We didn't have a clue where we were going or why these guns were pointed at our heads. My legs were bruised from the rifle butt that struck me. A trickle of blood ran from Peter's neck. I was ready for a commercial break and a glass of cold milk. But this wasn't TV.

When we finally arrived at a small outpost, we learned what we had done. We'd crossed into Spanish Sahara without knowing. This was the border patrol. It was serious. At the headquarters, a small clay hut in the desert, sat an official.

He was a mess of a man. If our fate lay with him, I was seriously worried. Even though he wore the uniform of an officer, with his ruthless laugh he had the attitude of an illiterate peasant. His cap and jacket were worn through with holes. His teeth were rotten and black. He smoked a chillum and drank sweet mint tea.

They kept us outside, with a guard looking over us. Peter looked scared.

Only half an hour had gone by when a woman appeared at the door. She was a small, pretty woman in jeans and a sweater. She had curly brown hair and wore lipstick the color of the sunrise. She eyed us sadly and asked if we spoke Spanish. I asked if she spoke English. Peter asked if she spoke Swedish. But there were no common languages until Peter struggled to ask if she spoke French, which she did. Neither of us could speak it, but we could understand a word or two.

She told us that she was the official's wife. Then came the bad news. She told us we had been arrested as spies.

Our robes and turbans, she said, made them think we were impersonating Arabs. And with downcast eyes she said that they were going to shoot us.

"Shoot us?"

Both Peter and I jumped at this thought.

"You mean, with bullets?" I said.

Only a few hours ago we had been dancing like fools on the dunes. And now this?

Then we learned of the tensions at the border between Morocco and Spain. There were armies and there was war. Our little morning walk had been a big mistake.

She began to cry. Things did not look good.

We stood there, shaking. *Shot for spying? No court, no judges, no jury?* If this was true, then we would be buried in the desert sands in our Moroccan garb. And no one would ever know.

We just sat down on the ground, swollen with pain, and feeling the seconds of our lives tick away.

The heat was now upon us and my lips were cracked from the dry air. My legs ached from the march. Peter was shaking, but the blood from his wound had dried on his neck. We looked at each other with question marks in our eyes.

At any moment we expected someone to set us free. But such was not the case. We could hear the brutal talk from inside, the voices desperate. The captain spoke in strong, forceful tones. The official was slow to anger, but it seemed as though a quarrel was taking place. Our pretty friend asked where we were born and if we were Christian.

She ran back to the men, perhaps to speak in our favor. We hung on every word, every nuance in her voice, straining to hear the response. But it didn't sound good.

Finally the captain came storming out of the hut with several men at his side. He was yelling orders.

Time began moving quickly, too quickly to protest or think of other options.

Soldiers raised us up. One wielded a knife, quickly slicing our ropes and freeing our hands. But this was not freedom. They shoved rifles in our backs and forced our hands to our heads.

The official came out of the building. He rocked on his heels and spat on the dirt with his hands on his hips. His wife began pleading, holding his arm, tears on her face. She yelled at the captain as he mounted his camel.

Peter was crying. I was, too.

They pushed and shoved us out toward a flat stretch of ground. More soldiers mounted their camels. We were forced to face the sun, side by side. The captain fired a shot in the air, sending terror through us.

We both now felt death coming. Our hands dropped to our sides, and the woman was screaming hysterically. The captain ordered everyone to mount his camel. Every remaining man swung up on his saddle and they all cocked their rifles in the air. The captain barked more orders and the men formed their camels into a semicircle, facing us. The camels were champing their bits restlessly.

I remember looking up the barrels of the guns as they were lowered at us.

Peter moved even closer to me. Our bodies pressed hard together, shoulder to shoulder, arm to arm, our fingers touching. We looked straight ahead while the captain ordered the guns readied.

I remember birds in the sky circling around and a cloud floating across the horizon. I noticed ants in the sand and an abandoned shoe on the dirt. An old cane leaned against the hut and a cross hung over the door.

I could smell Peter in my soul, his fear mixed with mine. Moments turned into long rivers of time, and fleeting thoughts took on lives of their own.

I looked at the men and could see them clearly. I could see their whiskers, one by one, the roots of their hair and the moles on their cheeks. I could smell the breath of the camels, hear their gurgling stomachs and shifting limbs.

I looked at the men again and could hear their thoughts.

And I could hear Peter thinking of me.

It was as if we could finally speak. I felt myself asking him if he loved me. I felt us talking in our heads. The guns were cocked and the sights steadied on our hearts. The barrels wavered in the air before taking accurate aim. The captain's voice barked a command. Our feet touched the desert and I could feel a drop of Peter's sweat on my arm. Even in Spanish, we knew what he was shouting.

"Ready!"

And the breathing was in sync between Peter and I. The last breath was drawn before the impact of lead.

"Aim!"

I felt Peter inside me, screaming my name. I could feel the desert consuming our bones and the birds singing our death song.

"Fire!"

A volley of bullets exploded all around, deafening us. Bullets whizzed through the air slightly above our heads and off toward the dune.

They had missed! And we were still standing!

Peter and I looked at each other, expecting another round.

With a loud whoop the captain shot his gun in the air, and then they all began shooting off bullets. They circled around, spitting in our faces. They circled once more. And then they raced away into the desert, laughing like dogs.

They left us alive. And free.

The woman came running up once they were gone. She cursed the captain and begged us to run back to our camp before he changed his mind.

She was shaking with relief and swore the captain was insane.

We agreed.

Peter and I sprinted across the desert. We ran faster than the wind. Finally we saw the encampment of cardboard boxes, a welcome refuge. We ran and ran until we were back in our box, safe from the border patrol.

14

Across the Sands to El Aaiún

Beginning that day—and for the next six—we never strayed more than a few yards from our box. The love we felt for it may have been the start of my lingering fetish for small spaces.

That night Peter and I ate sardines and chick-peas from the can. We had paid a visit to the old merchant at "the corner market" and bought a week's worth of packaged food. It was years beyond shelf life, but who were we to complain? At least we still possessed stomachs to feed and hearts that beat.

We huddled close together inside the box. The corner farthest from the door became our nook. We set booby traps of old rusty nails, scattering them at the entrance to foil midnight kidnappers or marauding border patrols. When we slept we lay in each other's arms. In our djellabas we slumbered fitfully under a blanket and shook like nervous rabbits. I kept seeing the barrel of a gun aimed at me every time I closed my eyes. And in his sleep Peter talked like a Swedish devil, sometimes punching into the air. We just held on tight and rode out the bad dreams.

For the rest of the week the cardboard village must have thought we were Siamese twins. Nothing could separate us. We took to walking back to back so we could see in all directions. And we began talking to each other in our native tongues despite the fact neither of us could understand a word of the other's. But in a way we really did.

I told Peter, while holding him in the dark and listening to his snoring, that all the oceans in the world couldn't keep us apart. I said all the rain in the sky wouldn't put out the fire I felt in my heart for him.

Of course he was asleep and couldn't hear me wax poetic into his perfect ears. While he slept I told him all the things I wanted to do with him. I said if he didn't look so much like the Jesus I'd seen on the back of every church singing book I might be shooting comets across his skin and sucking on his toes. I told him what a drop of pearly white heaven he was to me.

Sometimes when he was awake he'd sit there, looking at me deep in the eyes and holding my hand so tight that my fingers would go numb. He'd talk to me in a soothing voice in words I didn't understand. His eyes would water like a stream in a pouring spring rain. Who knows what he was saying to me? Might have been hockey scores or career plans. But it could have been passionate poems. At least that's what I hoped for.

We never did any touching under the robes. I guess we were afraid.

A week later the border finally opened again. More trucks arrived, but we never did see another dead goat. That was a relief. The contraband bandits were a crabby group of men, and all on edge about transferring all the cargo before the border captain arrived.

By week's end ten more young travelers had arrived. We felt like seasoned old warriors compared to their fresh-faced smiles. Peter and I stuck to ourselves, with only an occasional word of warning to them about taking needless strolls through the dunes.

On the day of the crossing we rose early to be the first in line. Precisely at eight, like the week before, we heard the rumble of the military bus coming in its cloud of dust.

It was the same square-jawed captain with the same sloppy crew of soldiers and the same ritual as before. We both felt an inner dread. This time we had a plan, though. We'd split Peter's money so we both had a fair share. I pinched my cheeks and tried to look as healthy as I could. And if that didn't work, we'd try a bribe.

Just as the gate opened, we turned to see another cloud of dust roaring up from behind. It was a Jeep speeding across the desert, making its way to the border. A few of the soldiers began to panic. But the Jeep pulled to a stop just in time and out hopped Henry, still in his suit and tie.

Peter and I were jumping up and down at the sight of him. He gathered up his bags, smiling and saying he was pleased to see us again. He started talking in his fractured pidgin English about his week-long hike through the desert and nearly losing his mind.

He saw Buddha, that's who he saw. And he'd resigned himself to dying.

Three days prior, the two burly French Moroccans in the Jeep had found him blabbering on a dune and rescued him. They fed him chocolate and Coca-Cola, bringing him back to life.

And there he was, suit and all, ecstatic to see the border.

The captain began barking orders for us to start moving through. Peter went first. He breezed through and flashed me a victory sign. When my turn came, the captain scowled and once again asked about my cholera shots. The money didn't matter. He barred me once again.

I was stunned. Peter stood helpless on the other side. Nothing I could say would change the captain's mind. He let everyone else in line through with no problem. When it became obvious that I was once again refused entry, Henry came to my rescue.

Henry had balls, even if he was only five feet tall. He walked right up to the captain and told him in no uncertain terms that I was his long-lost brother. The captain arched his brows. Henry ranted away in his broken Spanish with Japanese inflections. The soldiers stared on in disbelief. Everyone looked from me to Henry and could see plain as day that we weren't related. But Henry went on. He said we had different fathers but were on our way to see our dying mother. At this they all started howling with laughter.

The more he spoke, the more they laughed. But the captain wasn't moved. The bus started up and everyone was loaded on board. Henry got louder and his Spanish got worse. He began pleading and said that our mother would die of a broken heart if I didn't come. Then he started crying, sobbing in the captain's arms. Even I started to believe. Henry was yelling the name of the Holy Mother and crossing himself.

Well, that did it.

The captain didn't dare offend the Holy Mother. He finally stamped my passport, waved me through and sternly forbade Henry from saying another word in Spanish.

I boarded the bus not a moment too soon, and we took off for the great El Aaiún.

For the next several hours we rumbled along through the war zone. For all the rumors we'd heard, we didn't know a war this big was going on. The bus was stopped at a dozen military checkpoints. We all filed out one at a time to show our passports. Massive military encampments were spread throughout the desert. We didn't like the look of this.

By the time we arrived in El Aaiún it was nightfall. The streets were crowded with military personnel, trucks and tanks. Meanwhile, bombers streaked overhead. The city itself had paved streets and bright orange lights. Low, humble buildings lined the dusty, littered avenues.

The bus let us off in the town center, where we said goodbye to Henry. As I gave him a kiss, it dawned on me that I didn't know how he kept his suit and tie looking so nicely pressed the whole time.

But then he was gone, taking his secret away with him forever.

Peter and I didn't have a clue where to begin our search for Joseph. We began checking hotels, if you could call them that. They were really nothing more than run-down flophouses with a Spanish twist. On our fourth try we came to an end-of-the-alley hostel that someone said was the cheapest in town. We had a feeling Joseph was there.

The stucco exterior of the hostel was pitted with large holes. A pile of garbage sat against the building, and rats scuttled to and fro in the alley. It looked closed. A few soiled sheets were draped over two chairs in a room that passed for the lobby. Metal bars guarded the open window.

We pounded on the bars, but got no answer. Finally a man hobbled out from a back room. He was wearing Western clothes and had a dapper hat on his head. But his face was pitted like the surface of the moon.

He spoke no English, only Spanish and French. So once again we laboriously tried to communicate. Gesturing with his hands, in great detail Peter described Joseph to the clerk.

Finally a look of recognition spread over the clerk's face. He told us to wait a moment. He walked back through the door and soon we heard him speaking with another man. At last he reemerged with an envelope in his hand. Peter's name was on it and our faces lit up. It was a note from Joseph.

Joseph and Sylvia had flown to Tenerife in the Canary Islands, where they were waiting for us. This I learned by studying the map that Joseph had drawn.

We left the hotel, more confused then ever. None of it made sense. Why would they go to the Canary Islands when we all had agreed on heading south?

We were puzzled, but not for long.

Once we were back on the street, panic broke out and citizens and soldiers came running by. The town was on military alert. A battle was raging only twenty kilometers outside the city limits. Civilians were hurrying down the street, carrying bundles on their heads. Convoys full of soldiers were heading out of town.

We saw a military bus with other foreigners climbing on board. The driver said he was going to the airport. Tourists were advised to leave El Aaiún on the next flight.

We boarded the bus and saw the same people we'd traveled with from the border. But Henry was not among them.

Driving through the streets, the bus careened around corners, barely missing donkey carts. Pandemonium was in the air.

By the time we got to the airport there were military jets booming overhead. Inside the terminal we were herded to a makeshift counter to purchase tickets. The one flight out was going to Tenerife. Peter paid for the tickets, and within an hour we were boarding the plane.

Once we were on board, shock began to settle in. Weeks in the desert with crazy Moroccans, dead goats and firing squads, and now we were fleeing a war? Peter and I found two seats in the back, where no one could gawk at us. We knew what an ugly sight we were.

The plane was full of tourists from Madrid going to the Canary Islands for the Christmas holidays. And here we were, dressed in turbans, robes and sandals, with dirty faces, smelling of camels, looking starved and shell-shocked.

We sat in our seats and looked at each other. And suddenly we began rolling with laughter. We were lucky to be alive, and we looked like two madmen. Before we knew it, the plane was in the air.

Ten thousand feet up, listening to Muzak and drinking tea, we sat in a plane full of mom-and-pop tourists, saccharine-sweet stewardesses and the most godawful orange upholstery I've ever seen. The banality of the Western world was slowly sinking in.

I held Peter's hand. Only a night ago we had been shivering in a box on the desert floor.

Peter looked at me and smiled another godly smile. But I'd had enough sweet smiles. I wanted to rip off his robe, hump in our seats and wrestle some sweat out of his perfect brow. I was sick and tired of this tenderhearted touching. It was time to get naked and roll in the aisles.

I was in love.

We finally kissed. Not just a peck, but a real kiss, tongues and all. I could have climbed into his mouth and swallowed him whole. His controlled, cool demeanor finally came unglued and his lips tore at me like a slobbering dog. We were crazed, passionately making out under the cabin lights in the back of the plane. And damn if either of us cared who was watching.

Apparently half the plane was.

A stewardess finally came by and nudged us to stop. But I wasn't about to. This was the most long-awaited kiss of my life. Nothing was going to stop me.

He may have been a god, but at that moment he was no more than steaming mouth and passionate tongue. And we kissed and kissed until our lips were sore.

The plane trip was a blur. The stewardess finally gave up. By the time we got to Tenerife our male-bonding experience had gone as far as it dared. And I knew that somewhere on this island during the course of the night I would finally get laid by the King of the Swedes.

15

The Madman of Tenerife

We landed at the Tenerife airport, on a plateau above town, at ten in the evening. Outside the terminal taxis and buses clogged the road. It was nearly Christmas. Thousands of tourists jammed the curbs to catch a ride. We stood like lost sheep, not knowing where to go. The Western world was smacking us hard with its appalling speed. Finally a shuttle bus stopped at the curb and took us to Tenerife.

Half an hour later we were downtown. The city was packed. Bars and restaurants opened to the streets where drunken hordes staggered down the sidewalks. Cars streamed by, loud and honking. We had arrived at the busiest intersection in town. The bus took off, leaving a cloud of exhaust in which we stood clutching our bags like two street urchins. We'd had the sense to remove our turbans but were still in our dirty robes.

That's when I heard an American voice.

My ears instantly perked up. The mere sound of an American accent in the middle of Tenerife was music to my ears. I strained to look for its source amid the fast-moving cars.

Suddenly I saw him on the far corner. He was not an Ugly American but a Young American with a clever smile and a small goatee. He couldn't have been more than thirty and wore wire-rimmed glasses on his prominent nose. He was built like an ex-marine.

He stood gesturing in the air in front of a travel agency. His voice was piercing as a peacock's in the dead of night. Everyone who passed him listened for a second. He had a slight Southern twang. For a moment I thought him a Baptist preacher working for converts.

It had been so long since I'd seen an American. But his words were also vaguely intriguing.

Peter, not understanding a word, was immediately suspicious and did not want to go closer. I had to drag him with me across the street.

Half a dozen people were listening while he ranted about Christmas and its mystical meaning. He bounced into other topics, going in-depth on world politics. He was a nut.

Like any pontificator, it was his charm that held your attention. He was more like a poet, and he quoted Yeats or Shakespeare with a dramatic flair. Suddenly he spotted us and waltzed toward Peter, reciting a love sonnet of sorts. Peter cringed at the attention.

I started talking to him. His name was Tom. I was so happy to talk that I gave him the rundown of our past several weeks. Once he was aware of our plight, he insisted we stay in his hotel room.

I tried to explain to Peter that we had a place for the night. Peter didn't like this at all. Either he wanted me alone or he didn't like Tom, I wasn't sure. But Peter wouldn't budge. He wanted to find Joseph or another place to stay.

We finally compromised. Peter waited at a nearby cafe and I went with the American to look at the hotel. I said I'd be back soon.

I sealed the promise with a kiss and walked down the street with Tom. I turned and looked back at Peter, flashing him a wink and a smile. He looked at me with sad, watery eyes and blew me a kiss as if that were the last he'd see of me.

On the way, Tom commented about the window displays of every shop in town. He was at the same time brilliant and remarkably scattered.

By the time we arrived at his hotel I was beginning to feel the exhaustion of the day. I wanted to take a quick peek and go back to Peter back on the street.

The hotel was an elegant building in a state of slight disrepair. We passed the front desk, where a short, squirrely man was attending the books and didn't once look up to see who we were. The ceilings were high, with fans turning the air. Tall potted palms stood along the walls and I expected to hear birds.

I did. There were loud parakeets perched in a cage.

I instantly loved the place and wished Peter had come.

We took the stairs to the third floor. Tom's room was the last door in the corridor, separated from the others by a long breezeway. He unlocked the door, chuckled to himself and wished me a good stay.

I thought this strange, but went in anyway.

His room was a mess. Not a mindless mess but a psychotic mess. A bed frame leaned against the wall. The mattress was removed and lay on the floor, covered with sheepskins and wool carpets. Stacks of books lined the shelves.

The walls were covered with art. Not mature art, but

the art of the insane, as though a dozen very disturbed tots had been let loose with crayons.

Dozens of candles burned in the room, and hundreds more had seeped wax all over the floor. Clothes were strewn everywhere—costumes, women's clothes, men's clothes and hats. Dozens of them were nailed to the ceiling.

The room was large, almost a suite. Twenty feet by thirty, with one small window looking out on a brick wall. There was a toilet, but no tub. He said the communal bath was down the hall.

Once inside I felt alarm. The inside of his door had half a dozen bolts, which he speedily locked. I asked him why he had so many locks. He said one never knew who they might need to keep out, or in.

Walking around the room was not easy because of all the debris. He had a stereo on a table and stacks of tapes on the dresser. In the dresser was a gun.

That's when I started to moan.

Not a big moan, but a little baby whimper from the back of my throat.

He told me to shut up and for some reason I did.

His mood changed abruptly. "Sit down," he ordered me menacingly.

I told him I needed to get back to my friend and headed for the door.

He drew in a breath and pulled out the gun.

I couldn't believe it. I thought I was dreaming. Looking down the barrel of yet another gun now seemed like old hat to me. I told him he might as well just get it over with if that's what he was going to do. But he had other things in mind.

He put the gun back in the drawer.

Just as I was about to make a bolt for his keys, he grabbed a sword off a table. It was an Arabic scimitar, nearly three feet long, with an elaborate handle and curved steel blade.

That's when I laughed. Now I knew I was dreaming. But this was no sitcom.

He suddenly took a slice at a chair and splintered it in two. He then stood poised ready for me.

Well, maybe this wasn't a dream, I started to realize.

He sat me down in a chair and said my head was coming off if I made another sound.

I believed him.

He began ranting again. This time he went off about his favorite rock bands. All I could think of was poor Peter, down the street without a clue as to which hotel we'd gone to. I leaped for the door again.

That was a big, big mistake.

Tom was at my throat in a second and scratched the back of my hand with the blade. My blood welled up, thick and red. Now I had no doubt that he was a certifiable lunatic.

Then I got the full treatment.

He gagged me with electrical tape and bound my hands and feet. Then he pushed me down on the mattress.

This was no pleasant S-and-M bedroom scene. It was abduction plain and simple, and I was not impressed with his style.

For hours he ranted on about his mess of a life. I learned more than I wished to know. An AWOL marine? A fugitive from the law? A drug-smuggler and serial killer? I didn't know what to believe, he had so many tales.

He said he'd walked all the way from Asia to Africa

and had been branded in Iraq and raped in Algiers. When he rolled up his sleeves, it did in fact look like he had seen a branding iron.

I was sufficiently convinced. He was a dangerous man.

Then he put on Jimi Hendrix. I like Jimi Hendrix and always have. But to Tom, Jimi was religion.

That rant lasted into the wee hours of the morning. He had written twenty poems to the man, and I had to hear them all.

He was looped on crystal meth. In between his rants he was razor-blading speed on a mirror and taking good, healthy snorts. My job was to listen, and listen I did—to every word. If I didn't, he'd hit me on my head with the back of his sword.

I was getting a really bad headache.

He had money all over the room from smuggling hashish, and by the looks of things had been spending it as well. All the trinkets scattered around were going back home to his folks in North Carolina.

On and on he talked.

He had a very captive audience—there was nothing I could say with the tape over my face. He liked that just fine.

Finally, in the morning, he went out. The moment he was gone I was banging on the wall as hard as I could. Then I tried the old rub-the-ropes-against-the-edge-of-a-mirror trick.

That's when he returned.

He was not happy with me—no, not at all.

He stood me up in a corner and cranked up his music as loud as he could. He started to torture me. Slow and deliberate. With the tip of his sword. Not hot. Not sexy. Blood-curdling and sadistic, and I was filled with terror.

Round and round with the tip of his sword he played with my nerves. Three strokes and my robe fell to the floor, along with some of my skin. He poured scalding hot wax over my head till my eyes blistered from pain.

He loved to see me twitch and moan.

He tightened my ropes like a tourniquet until my hands were bright and blue. He poked my chest like a pincushion and twisted my ears.

And then came the floor show.

"Time for purification," he said.

I was kneeling in bloody pain, waiting for that sword to come ripping through my head.

Instead he opened his bottom drawer and took out a huge container of Johnson & Johnson's talcum powder.

He was totally psycho, mumbling to himself.

He began sprinkling talcum powder all over me. Head to toe, everything got the treatment. I was as white as a zombie, kneeling on the floor, choking on the powder, barely able to breathe. Then he went wild all over the room until everything was snow-white—the rugs, the sheepskins, the bed, the clothes, the closet, the toilet. He had more than a case of baby powder and he emptied it all.

Then he did himself. He was John the Baptist and I the new Christ, he said. He gave himself a good powdering, but he skipped his face. He snorted more speed. For his next trick he began blowing crystal meth up my nose through a straw.

Now I was looped too.

He powdered the walls and went streaking around the room. He was crazy on speed. He pulled off his pants and started dancing on the table, babbling incoherent garbage in the air.

A go-go boy he was not.

He finally sat in the corner for nearly an hour, mumbling to himself. He ranted more on the theme of John the Baptist, the Garden of Eden and good curry recipes that he'd tried overseas.

I couldn't keep up and drifted away trying to block out his words. I prayed for sitcoms to enter my brain.

There on the floor, bound, covered in powder, Jimi Hendrix blaring in my brain...

Time became irrelevant. Time in fact stood still. There was no time.

He began to dress and undress, exploring his own inner hell. He play-acted characters from a private world. Every time he turned around he had a new rant and a new costume.

And by the second day I wanted to kill.

On that day he had a very serious talk with me. Sort of man-to-man. He sat me up in a chair and said my time had come.

He wanted to test my faith. I felt old-time religion coming on. I felt Bibles, hell and brimstone. Baptism by fire.

But to him, Hendrix was God. If I were a true believer, then I was supposed to know, in one word what Hendrix was singing about.

He whispered this demand into my ear. I was so unbalanced from drugged and sleepless nights, with no food and bleeding wounds, that it all made sense. I knew exactly what he wanted.

For the next several hours I listened carefully to every last tape that Hendrix ever made.

I heard things that I'd never heard before.

Hendrix and I became one.

Tom stood over me with his sword. He said he had one question and that I'd die if I answered wrong. If I was right, I would get to live with him in this room.

I voted for the latter. I listened and listened, rocking on my heels. Near the end of the day, as Jimi would say, I was experienced.

Tom turned off the stereo. He stood before me in an Elizabethan-era costume, his lips red and a tiara on his head. He anointed me with more talcum powder and in a grand gesture ripped off my gag, taking half my lips with it.

I breathed in deeply and looked up at Tom, or John the Baptist or whatever he was. He stood poised in the air with his sword pointed at my throat. His lips were pursed when he asked, "Well, what's the message behind Jimi's songs?"

I shrugged and made a good stab. "I dunno. His mom, I guess. He's singing about his mom?"

He looked at me like I'd just uttered the most profound piece of wisdom the world had ever known. His lips mouthed the word "Mom" over and over. First slowly, then furiously. He began yelling "Mom!" and laughing maniacally. He started spinning around the room, chanting. He sang at the top of his voice for all the "Moms" in the world.

And then he collapsed on his bed, out like a light.

I just stood there wondering what that was all about. I really didn't get it. I waited for him to move, kind of hoping he was dead. But he wasn't. He just lay twitching in a sleep that could last for days.

When I saw he was out for good, I cut off my ropes against the edge of his sword.

I found my robe and my bag. I grabbed some of his money, too. I took his keys and began unlocking the bolts. Then I cracked open the door and charged out of the room.

I ran down the stairs and stopped at the front desk. There I told the sleepy Spanish clerk that there was a psycho in a room upstairs. I begged him to call the police. But as I spoke he looked at me like *I* was the psycho. I realized he might have a point. Covered in baby powder, with wax on my head and after no sleep for days, I was looking the part.

I was over the edge.

So I ran out into the street. It was late in the day, but over the next few hours I searched for Peter. I went to the cafe. No one remembered him.

I began searching hostels and hotels. But he was not lodged anywhere. No one knew of him.

I cried on the streets of Tenerife.

A young Irish woman took pity on me. She said to try the bulletin board at the post office, that maybe he'd left a note.

I rushed downtown, flying through traffic. I made it just in time, just before they locked the doors.

There on the board was an envelope with my name on it. I grabbed it and ripped it open. I held a fragile piece of paper in my white baby-powder hands.

And on it, in English, read these words: "Michael. I fly to Senegal. Why have you disappeared from me? I will always love you. Peter."

PART THREE

16

Down East to Maine

I am a fool.

I'm sitting in the back car of a train bulleting over the tailored green patchwork of Connecticut. I stare out the window at images that whizz by in a fade of gray. Every seat's full of briefcase-clutching Wall Street clones returning to their picket-fenced abodes. And I chew on a brownie that Annie Sprinkle gave me for the trip. I left her in New York after the march on Washington.

I don't know why, but here I am on my way to New England to visit Chris, the man with no penis. He left one message, just a few scratchy words, on my voice mail.

"Mike. I need you, man. Come find me in Portland," he'd said in a warm but rootless-sounding voice. "I need someone to hold."

I'd listened to it over and over till I could repeat it backward if I had to. I'd almost forgotten about him, but not quite.

He *would* have to say the magic word: "need." It plugs me in when someone says that word because I adore being needed. So it didn't take much to get me off on another foolish chase for love. And all I've got is a number to call when I get there.

The South Station clock says five and Boston's but a brownstone amusement park. I check the bus schedules to Portland, Maine, and see I have over an hour to kill.

Rain soaks the cobblestones. I surf across the streets of Bean Town, drenched and duck inside the Club Cafe with its ultra-white urban crowd.

This place is a shade more tony than my road-weary self can endure. Sensing my displeasure, a drag queen of a hostess sends me packing across the river to check out the basement at Paradise Two. "Lots of dirty old men! You'll love it," she says, arching her penciled brows.

After crossing the Charles by bus, I bound out, slip on the curb and land at the door of Paradise Two. While a herd of improper Bostonians politely sidesteps this catastrophe, I fix my eyes upon a flier posted on the wall. It announces the club's retro-orgasmic seventies shoe sale for the benefit of a gay and lesbian center.

Examining the half-inch hole in one of my shoes I know this must be my ticket to podiatric bliss. I waltz indoors in search of my very own pair of pre–Doc Marten disco platforms with cork soles.

Inside, the stage is covered with dozens of unisex pairs of footwear. A not-so-sober cast of high-heeled queens is pressed against the wall, all waiting for their turn to model shoes on the runway. Two attitude queers in leather and lace are spit-polishing the heels of their boots.

The mistress of ceremonies, with her vegetable-enhanced headdress, is whipping the crowd into a purchasing frenzy. Hoofing her way around the stage in a pair of four-inch platforms with floral upholstery, she exalts the virtues of the square toe. While she goes on I feel my own toe being squared off by a punk dyke with a wicked instep.

"Excuse me, I think you're stepping on my toe," I say with a grimace.

She appraises me and then deliberately grinds her black felt platform shoe deeper into my foot and points to a sticker on the lapel of her leather jacket that reads CAUTION: DO NOT PLAY ON OR AROUND! I squirm, trying to free my toe from the weight. I look down at my throbbing foot and her spindly leg. She is young and raunchy, chewing on a straw. I can smell her breath and see the veins on her neck. She isn't about to budge. And just as I consider dumping my drink on her head, she leaps up to the stage. This is my chance to retreat to the basement.

The basement scene is at a standstill. Not a single dirty old man to be found. And considering the presence of M.I.T.'s nuclear reactor, a mere stone's throw across the street, there is a surprising absence of mutants.

I stand against the wall, nursing my toe while remaining on the lookout for the wound-up dyke in black leather. A few preppy Harvard types slosh down their beers next to three green-lipped boys who are kissing the wall and leaving lipstick imprints around the room. I change my mind. The mutants are here after all.

Then *she* appears!

The dyke with a toe to grind comes clomping across the room in even bigger clodhoppers. The back of her jacket reads FUCK WAR, and I have the paranoid delusion that when she looks at me she sees the very picture of a hawk.

Maybe she's just looking around for bigger feet to grind. I'm only a size ten, after all. But she makes a beeline right for me.

I feel it coming. The shoe. The crunch. The toe pressing mine into the floor. I already hear myself screaming. I wait as she comes closer. Then she is by my side, grinding my toe deep into the basement floor. The room spins in a mad dance frenzy of green-lipped boys and sloshed preppies high on speed.

It's definitely time to leave.

I find my way back to the depot to board the six-thirty bus for Portland. I should get a frequent rider award this year for so many bus miles. A free ticket to Portland, Oregon would do just fine.

It's not a long ride, but it's a slow one. We chug north in the mist through Newbury, Portsmouth, Kittery and Kennebunk. The salt air and salted roads bear evidence to the winter past; rust eats at every car in sight: rusty holes, creaky doors, corroded bumpers, decaying floorboards, rusted hoods, mirrors, door handles...rust eats at any protrusion, corrupting chrome and metal with its insatiable burnt-orange tongue, constantly on the move for fresh metal.

A disproportionate number of Dodge Coronets go screeching by, dragging their rusted entrails on the road, sending sparks into the air. The low-riders are further encumbered by an equally disproportionate number of big people. Not portly, not Rubenesque, but big, really, really big people in Spandex pants and double-knit tops with midsections that bounce over frost heaves in the road.

The farther north we travel, the wider the bottoms and the rounder the bellies. Bottoms that spread across two car seats, stomachs that crease under the curve of the steering wheel, chins that fold into mounds of flesh.

I press my face against the frosted window, looking

down at a passing Coronet, its tires nearly flattened by its payload. A family of four sit inside like giant water balloons, completely filling it. I think of my bony butt, my protruding ribs, my knobby knees.

How'd they do it? I'm wondering.

Their car accelerates down the hill, leaving a trail of sparks. A hand tosses an empty Bud out the window.

Guess the answer's in the can.

Lobster signs rise out of the fog like beacons on a misty asphalt sea. The bus is hugging the Atlantic on Route 1, sailing by small seaside villages with their piers, fishing boats and low-tide inlets sheltering mussels and clams there for the picking. They call it Down East even though we're far north of Boston.

Near sunset, the bus parks adjacent to a dock where a lobster pound is doing a brisk business. We stop for twenty-minutes. I get out and take a stroll by the wharf, where lobster traps are stacked six high. Small fishing boats circle the bay, checking the brightly colored buoys that mark their traps on the ocean floor.

A kid who doesn't look a day over nineteen is thirty yards from shore in a small outboard motorboat, tending family traps. He has red hair, freckles and forearms made of steel. His thick hands are ungloved, and beneath a yellow poncho and cap his deep blue eyes burn icy holes in the shoreside gawkers who yell inane questions at him. He is struggling to pull up a trap and obviously annoyed about being such a spectacle.

"How much does that trap weigh?" asks a platinum blonde in a pink leisure suit.

"Can lobsters bite?" her girlfriend asks.

Ignoring the questions, he continues pulling on the stubborn rope. Something is caught below. Mustering all his strength, veins popping out of his forearms, he finally lifts the trap out along with its catch. Several ladies clap as he grabs a lobster, bands its claws, tosses it in a bucket, and rebaits the trap with rotten herring. The trap splashes into the sea again, uncoiling its ropy length until an orange buoy bobs up to the surface.

I am sufficiently enticed and keep watching along with the crowd.

He floors the outboard across the water to the next trap. A mother of three in a sailor cap yells, "How many does that make? Do you have to work in the dark?"

By now he is really irritated. Close to a dozen flatlanders are watching from the dock, sipping steaming coffee. The women are thrilled watching this young buck pull at the buoys, his neck glistening with sweat, his ungloved hands blue from the cold sea. He is the main attraction in the bay.

"He's sexy!" the pink-suited lady whispers to her friend.

I silently agree, but wish they'd stop bothering the poor guy. After another catch, the flatlanders thunder more questions from the dock.

"How much does it weigh?" someone yells.

"Assholes," I see the kid mutter under his breath, his face flushed with anger. The job is obviously taking longer than he'd hoped. Two more traps to go and he'll be out of this scene.

"What happens if you get caught in the line?" shouts the husband of the pink-suited lady.

The boy finally turns to answer. "Ya drown," he says in a thick Down East accent. "That's wut happens. You sink to the bottom of the bay and croak."

He was talking!

Everyone on the pier perks up and the women begin flirting.

"Do you make enough money at this to support a family? Do you have a family?"

I am fascinated by this exchange. Then suddenly I notice a small black-and-pink logo on the bow of the kid's boat that reads SILENCE = DEATH. I do a double take and strain for a better look at the sticker. And then I notice the pink triangle.

"Oh, my God!" I gasp and unconsciously push past the small crowd down to the dock's edge.

I stand cross-eyed for a moment, blinking the fog out of my eyes. *A born-in-the-salt fisherman, roughing the cold waters off the coast of Maine, is a queer?* I feel like I've discovered an oxymoron and throw a hard look across the water.

He works even faster now, wanting to be away from our needless distractions and finish his job.

"How long do you think you'll be doing this?" yells the pink-suited lady one more time.

Throwing in his last trap, the young fisherman grips the rudder, cranks the engine and in a sudden dramatic sweep around a buoy yells back, "When I find me a rich husband, I'll be outta here!" and speeds off into the twilight.

But this goes over everyone's head. They trade puzzled glances and leave the dock in the approaching night.

I go back to the bus.

Half an hour later we're pulling into downtown Portland. I've got my face mashed to the window, trying to see past the reflection of myself out to the streets.

Portland's a sleepy-looking town. Brick warehouses

stack close together in an old-as-the-Pilgrims neighborhood. A few cafes and eateries line the street, and I'm half expecting Chris to just be walking along looking for me. But he isn't.

At the bus station I'm glad I don't have a place to go. I can just drift out to the waterfront and its old docks and buy myself a cigar. I come across an old tavern on the corner of the oldest, meanest and coldest-looking street in town. It's on the water and they have stogies.

This does just fine. I wander into the bar to use the phone before buying myself a smoke. The place reeks of piss, cigars and men drowning in gin. The walls are oily to the touch and green linoleum curls up off the floor. Men hunch over their drinks, smoke streaming out of their nostrils, while a lone pool shark smacks balls across the felt-topped table, pocketing the eight.

I dig out my crumbled piece of torn-in-two paper and dial the number Chris left for me.

It's a motel. Figures.

A bitter old voice answers the phone and I don't remember Chris's last name.

"Sorry, no one here named Chris," the voice crackles, spitting up some evil phlegm.

"Well, maybe he's not under that name."

"Can't help ya without the right name."

I spend a minute describing his long hair, honey-brown eyes, smooth face, funny walk and big canyon smile that could blind a nun from a mile away. The clerk's listening to me and I can hear her shaking her head, no, until I come to the part about his walk. She's tapping her fingernails clickity click on the counter, I can hear it through the phone.

"Ayup. I know who ya mean," she says flatly. "I'll deliver a message."

"But can't he come to the phone?"

"No, sirree, he can call ya from the pay phone. What's your number?"

I look at the pay phone and it's one of those stinking deals that won't let you receive a call. I hate that. I tell her the tavern I'm at and she says she'll deliver the message.

I take a seat at the bar, buy myself a bad-ass cigar and toss the wrapper on the floor. It's so cheap I'm gagging before I even light it. I lean down across the bar, snatch up a pack of matches and look at the million and one postcards on the wall. Some old-looking ones from Amarillo, Texas, stare me in the face. One's from the Cadillac Ranch and shows a dozen Cadillacs sticking in the air. I puff on my cigar and wonder who sent all of these postcards.

Chris walks in. He's a lot taller than I remember and shocks me with a new buzz cut. Another quarter inch and he'd be as bald as me. His face looks drawn and heavy, with big circles under his eyes.

Walking his funny walk, he comes charging at me with more hurt in his face than I'd ever seen. Before I could even get up off the stool he's bear-hugging me like the world's about to end. I can feel his heart pitty-pat a mile a minute and his palms are sweating like a steam-room wall. He pulls me off my seat.

"Mike! Thank God you came. Quick, let's go," he says with a wild shake in his voice.

"Hey, hold on, man. What's the hurry?"

"Don't ask. I'll tell you in the van."

"What van?" I stub out the cigar and take big long

strides to keep up with him out on the street. His legs are moving like Jell-O over the cobblestones. We cross a few tracks where the trains used to run. We come up to the side of a green-and-yellow VW bus. He stops and opens the door.

"Chris, are you okay?" I ask. "What's up? You look like shit."

"Just get in. I don't know where to start. I mean, the past five days have been *bad.*"

"What's so bad?"

"It's Claudia and Helen. They're gone."

I moan. I definitely don't want to hear any more about those two. "You mean they left town?"

Chris's eyes twitch in his head like they're about to pop out. "They totally disappeared."

This sounds like good news to me. "Maybe it's for the best, Chris. Like, time to get on with your life."

Chris turns over the engine, pops in a tape and puts the van in gear. We spin out of there, across town and away from the bay. He's swerving around corners a little too fast.

"Uh, where we going? What's going on?" I ask.

His cheeks puff in and out like he's blowing up a balloon. "Okay. I, like, got up here late last Friday and walked up Brighton to Claudia's place. But she wasn't there anymore and no one knew where she'd moved. The next morning I bought this van and headed for Helen's boat. But when I got there, it was gone. Nothing left but garbage.

"This one old guy said the boat burned last winter. It burned like a firebomb. Flames were leaping out the windows and the whole thing burnt to the water. And dig this…it was Christmas Day. You know what day that was? That was the day I cut off my penis in El Paso.

"Well, they didn't find any bodies. The old guy said

he'd seen two women drive off early that morning. I know it was them. They've totally disappeared."

Chris's foot presses to the metal, barreling the bus up the highway. He's rattled to his bones and gripping the wheel like he's flying a fighter plane. I don't know what to say.

"Sorry," is the best I can do as I fidget in my seat, smelling gas fumes. "Sounds like it's time to just forget about them."

Chris doesn't even hear me. "Anyhow, I went to the P.O. box that me and Claudia used to share. There were a few pieces of mail. I found this one envelope from the police addressed to Claudia. I opened it and found her wallet and keys. I guess she'd lost them.

"In her wallet was this tiny address book. I'd never seen it before."

Chris fumbles in his coat pocket and tosses me a black book whose pages are embossed in gold. The edges are frayed and worn, and the binding's fallen apart. On the front, written in red, it says "Helen's Circle."

"What's in it?"

"Look," he says.

I open it and flip through the pages. There's hardly a single name inside.

"It's practically empty," I say.

"That's just it. There's five names in there. And the addresses are all over the country. I bet Helen and Claudia are with one of those people. I'm going to track them down somehow."

"You're totally out of your mind. Is that where you're going now?"

"Yeah. The first one's up in Belfast. That's where we're heading."

"We?"

"Well, you're here, aren't you?" Chris is rapping his fingers on the dusty dash.

"You're crazy, Chris. Is this why you wanted me to come up here?"

"I want to find out who these people are. And I wanted you to help me."

I'm smacking my gums, riding the horizon with my eyes. What am I doing, traveling Down East with this man? And now we're going to see a cult of God-knows-what in the backwoods of Maine? This isn't cool with me anymore.

"Chris." I clear the agitation out of my throat. "Listen. Pull over and let me out. I don't want any part of this. It's all your thing. Okay?"

He throws me a look like a deer caught in the lights. "What do you mean? Don't you want to help me find them?"

"No. Not really." I'm already wishing I was on a train going west.

"Then why'd you come?"

"Why'd you ask me to come?" I answer.

"I wanted you to help me."

"What about the 'I need someone to hold' part? That's what you said on your message."

"I just meant I need someone around."

"Brother, go hire yourself a private eye if you just want any old somebody around. You think I want to go hunting for two crazy women who kill chickens, drink blood and burn boats to the waterline? Hell, no. I came here because even if you don't have a dick I sort of like you. The main reason I'm sitting here right now is because you are one hell of a sweet man, with a *very* compelling smile. You're one of the most truly psychotic people I've ever met, so you can see what that says about me coming all the way up here to see you. What's the deal—you going to let me out so I can get to Portland?"

Chris rubs his eyes, wrinkles his nose and a big puzzled look comes on his face.

I wait for him to pull over.

"I'll get you back to Portland tomorrow," he says painfully.

"No, I mean Portland, Oregon. That's where I'm headed. I've got to get back out West. You just pull over here now. I'll stick out my little-bitty thumb just like you did when I met you. I'll get there on my own, thank you."

"I'll take you there, Mike."

"You'll what?"

"I'll take you to Oregon. Just do me this one favor, man. I can't go see these people alone...Please?"

"Absolutely not. Let me out!"

We pull over to the side of the winding road to Belfast, crickets echoing in the weeds. I don't know why, but I let him talk me into staying and we crash in the back of the van. Half hour to sunrise and we're curling up on a splintered platform of a bed under a pile of new blankets that smell like their cellophane wrappers. Chris is twitching in the dark, shaking like a box of rubber bands. I wonder if I'm ever going to live a normal life...ever.

17

Big Dog, Big Tongue

Morning comes and goes without us noticing until a logging truck rattles our bones awake. Chris lies across the bed, under the covers. I notice that all the soap in the world could never get all the filth out of here.

For a guy with loads of dough, he sure travels in squalor. The bus is a rat trap. A long line of ants crawl across the wall, headed for a pack of melted cheese. It's Velveeta and I feel hunger.

Chris rolls awake at the sound of another heavy log truck. He gives me a wink and thanks me for staying. I hold my head and realize I have a smoking headache from last night's cigar.

And I don't feel rested at all.

In his sleep, Chris chattered like an auctioneer at a barn sale. He's a class-A sleeptalker if I've ever met one. His legs kicked like a rodent against my back all night and I'm feeling a bit sore. But I forgive him.

I prop my chin against the window and breathe circles of fog on the glass. We're parked high on a bluff and the thick salty smell of ocean comes in through the door. One more truck rocks the ground and we're wide-eyed awake, looking at the clock.

"We gotta get going, Mike, don't you think?"

"I don't really want to get going, but we might as well get this business over with."

I pull on my Sunday-best pants, the slime-green ones, with a red flannel shirt that my cousin gave me last year. I put on the same old shoes I've worn for two decades and tie the laces together in a knotted mess.

Chris pushes open the door and we look out at the bay below. I make one more attempt to try to reason him out of this mad pursuit because it seems like it will lead nowhere.

But he's not changing his mind.

We drive into Belfast and stop at the first roadside food joint we come to. I love this place. They serve breakfast all day. The heady smell of coffee wraps around my nose and pulls me through the door.

We have hunger on our breath. I follow Chris as he shuffles in. I like his walk—it speaks of character, like he's carrying a loaded gun in his pocket. Sliding into the booth, I sit on a spot of ketchup and ruin my pants even before they had a chance to begin the day.

Outside the rounded window the street makes a lazy curve through the town. It's so New England picture-perfect that I half expect the Pilgrims to come riding up the lane.

The menu's printed on the placemat in front of us. Our waitress tiptoes over with water and coffee. She has a tight-as-a-harness apron around her tiny waist and isn't smiling. She might as well have a cigarette dangling off her lower lip because smoke is still drifting out her nose.

I like her chipped but blue-polished nails. I bet Chris

ten dollars that the snail-gray Pontiac parked out front is
hers, which turns out to be true.

The cook's not happy today. When I see an order of
eggs return to the kitchen, I decide it's time for lunch, not
breakfast. Chris orders half a pie from the round glass
pastry display next to the register, its FRESH BAKED sign
worn and old. The pie looks like it's been there for a year,
but Chris doesn't care one bit.

"What's the blue-book value of that thing you got
parked out there in the road?" our waitress asks when she
plops down our food.

"Twelve hundred, but I paid a thousand," Chris says.

He might as well have stood up on the counter and
made an announcement, because nearly two thirds of the
diner start going off about what a bad deal he got.

An old toothy guy in pale-colored pants that stick to
the back of his calves says he thinks the U joints are going
bad. Another tall guy with a thick neck and pimply nose is
folded up on a stool, disagreeing. He says the drums are
about to go. Doesn't matter what *we* think. Chris's van
becomes common property for discussion over the next
half hour.

A tall-as-tall-can-be woman enters the diner with no
less than six kids pulling on her flowery spring dress.
They all look like they've been dropped on their heads.
She carries a little paddle with her in case things get out of
hand.

"Whose van's that?" she asks.

Everyone in the whole damn place turns looking at us.

"Where ya going?" the oldest kid asks.

Chris pulls out the tiny address book, flips through
the pages and lands on the first name marked in red.
"Davenport, first name's Cole. We're looking for him."

No one's ever heard of him, despite the fact his place is only fifteen miles out of Belfast.

Chris reads the highway number and a few begin to nod their heads as though they've just realized who Cole Davenport is.

"Oh, you mean the one with the stumps," says the waitress.

Suddenly everyone gives a knowing nod.

"Wonder what kind of stumps he has?" I say to Chris.

We have ourselves each a tall, frosted mocha milkshake and split a roast beef sandwich. Then we go find the name in the book.

Cole Davenport lives way out in the sticks.

After an hour of off-road driving we pull up two miles of bumpy dirt road, soft with mud, and come upon a corrugated-metal building that looks like a barn. Machine and car parts are scattered like metal tombstones all across the field. We drive through a maze of tires piled to the sky.

Chris's heart pounds under his white thermal lumberjack's top. A locomotive-sized logging truck stacked high with logs is parked against the other side of the garage. And a crane twice the size of the barn perches like a praying mantis overlooking the carnage.

We pull up alongside a three-quarter-ton Chevy pickup with a rifle rack in the rear window when two black-as-pitch dogs come racing out to greet us. We'd be dead if our doors weren't closed. They grind their teeth against the metal and growl like gravel in a hurricane.

Chris honks his horn, brave as a Cherokee, and stares at the ten-foot-tall door to the corrugated barn.

A face finally looks out through a pane of glass two stories up. It's a flat-nosed face. The eyes are narrow and set close together.

After some time, the lower door of the building scrapes open across a concrete floor, making a horrible sound. A short person steps out, wearing no shirt at all. But this is no man. It's a woman.

She's got pearly white skin, blotched like sunbursts, flat saggy breasts and nipples on her chest the size of green olives. Her tits are so close together they look like a pair of crossed eyes.

She looks like she could tear a moose in half, and she isn't the least bit friendly. But this isn't a social call.

She yells at us in a gargled gulp, swallowing either chew or spit, we don't know which. "What you guys want here?"

I know what I want. I want to crawl under the seat and make this whole scene disappear.

"Looking for Cole Davenport," Chris yells through the crack in his window.

"Ayup, I'm Cole alright." Her veins bulge as she kicks her way past the door and hobbles out across the junk pile. She wears mail-order pants, blue just like in the pictures, and cut off ragged at the knees. Then we see her legs. Actually there are no legs, just two stumps. She's walking on wooden peg legs.

Across the mess of cars she strides on her pegs, with her nose flaring and snot dripping down the sides. She looks like she's going to smash a fist to the glass, she's so loaded. I look at Chris, cursing the road that brought us here.

Legless Cole comes over to the van and mashes her face against the windshield like a fresh-killed deer and says, "What the hell do you want with me?"

We sit there a second like we're at a drive-in movie eating popcorn on a warm spring day. Looks like a scary monster flick and we're wondering what's going to happen next.

Chris seems fearless except for the small beads of sweat on his brow. But I'm already anticipating early retirement once those two dogs of hers get their teeth in me.

"Just thought you might know the whereabouts of two friends of mine. Two women. I haven't seen them in a while."

Cole arches her brow. "What makes you think I'd know any friends of yours?"

"Their names are Claudia and Helen. You know them?"

"Who?"

"Claudia and Helen. One's about thirty. And the other's pretty old, wears her hair all tied up on the top, has a big mole on her forehead."

Cole snorts but doesn't say anything.

"I thought maybe you'd know because we found your name in their address book."

"What?" Suddenly Cole's face is off the glass and looking redder than blood.

"What?" she yells again, loud enough to set the dogs to barking and pounding her mean fist on the front of the van. "Who's got my name in a book?"

I tell Chris to slam it in reverse and get out of here. The dogs are up to the glass, snarling in our faces. Cole's neck veins twist like bridging cable before suddenly a look of revelation comes across her face. She backs away a bit, nodding.

"Oh, you talking 'bout queen Helen. Old Helen. Yeah. I know who you're talking about, with the big mole on her head."

We're shaking our heads up and down. Chris is saying, "Yeah, that's her," and Cole's nodding her head. The dogs are bouncing around now, all excited, as the wind whips up fistfuls of debris across the car graveyard.

Cole says, "Shut her down and come on in."

Chris and I shrug. Cole stilts across the rubbish back into the corrugated barn.

The dogs sit close to the van and we slowly exit. I tuck my hands firmly in my pocket to keep my fingers from their mouths.

Inside the barn it's a heavy-metal scene, with car engines everywhere. Cole grunts from above and we see a set of stairs leading off to the right. They're covered in grease, with no side rails to hold on to.

Her peg legs clomp on the floor above. We enter through a narrow door that leads into a green room. Green linoleum runs across the floor, up the walls and over the ceiling. Not quite the way I might have done it had it been mine, but a justifiable use of America's favorite floor covering.

The wall is hung with old calendars of naked girls and a shoddy attempt at a watercolor by an unsteady hand. Cole is sitting in a big old doghair-covered chair in the darkest corner of the room. A K-mart heater blows toasty air. Mail-order catalogs are stacked everywhere.

On a Formica tabletop are piles of old books and on the floor is The Dog. Not another black-as-death snarling dog but a Saint Bernard, big as an elephant and curious as a cat.

"Have a seat," Cole says to us.

As we sit on a couch that is matted with doghair and reeks foul as a swamp, we carefully avoid a few fresh turds steaming on the floor. We hope they're the dog's.

"So, you a friend of Helen's?" Cole is saying.

"Yeah. But I've lost touch with her and my friend Claudia. You know where she is?"

"I can tell you where she isn't." Cole leans across her armrest. "She ain't here, because if she was I'd set my dogs on her." A gurgling laugh comes out of her throat and she spits on the floor. "That witch cost me my legs."

We look down at her legs and up again. I wish she'd put on a shirt because every time I look her way I can't see past her green-olive nipples. She knows I'm stuck there looking, too.

"How do you know Helen?" Chris carefully asks.

"I used to fix her car back when she lived up here. Before she got the boat. She was nothing but an old witch, full of trouble. Every time I saw her she'd mess with my head. She never had money but I'd fix it for her anyhow. For repayment she'd tell my fortune, like I really needed to know.

"One night there was a really bad freeze and she couldn't get her car going. I got in the truck and went to give her a jump. On my way back I blew a rod six miles from here. I took off in the dark walking down the road, but the snow started in. I got so lost I couldn't make my way. I was out there for half the night and got frostbite on both legs. They had to amputate them. Wasn't for her I'd have 'em today."

Chris is nodding his head and I know he's thinking the same cursed thought about Helen. If it weren't for her, he might still have something *between* his legs.

Chris starts in on his whole bloody story and Cole settles back in her chair. Cole looks like she's heard it all before and doesn't flinch a muscle at the gory details.

While Chris talks, the old Saint Bernard gets up,

nearly four feet tall on all fours, and comes over to me. His tongue is a big sponge of wetness just pouring dog slobber all over the room. He stands dripping a gallon a minute on my legs and shoes.

I'm drenched in dog slobber and feel nausea coming on.

The room smells like a bad turkey dinner and I notice a plate of old green Jell-O. It sort of matches the room.

Cole cracks open a fifth of Jack Daniel's and guzzles at it like she's sucking on a baby bottle, barely coming up for air. The dog, who is named Charlie, just won't stop with me.

"I love your dog, but what's with all the slobber?" I finally interrupt.

"Oh, he's a little slow upstairs, if you know what I mean," she chortles heavily while pulling whisky through her lips.

I push away the dog.

Chris tries to find clues about where Helen might be. He's asking why Cole's name is in Claudia's book.

"Hell if I know!" says Cole, pounding one wooden leg on the linoleum. She turns on the radio and finds a top-forty station.

There is no end to Charlie's affections for me. Chris doesn't even notice.

Cole is cracking peanuts, tossing the shells on the floor.

I hold in my stomach. Things start to spin. It's a world of green linoleum and I see a slug crawling up the wall. That's when I heave. My whole lunch, mocha shake and all, spurts over the couch and onto the floor.

The elephant-sized dog wanders over and starts lapping it up. Charlie's snorting and grunting, wagging his house-sized tail, knocking over a lamp and sweeping aluminum cups off the tabletop. He's down there licking up every drop, which just makes me heave even more.

His massive tongue then begs at my face, lapping across my chin. I push him away.

Cole is sitting back in her chair, choking with laughter.

Chris pats me on the back and rubs my head.

I need a drink of water but the sink's got dishes in it looking older than dirt. A mold patch the size of an army grows up the wall into the faucets. While I sit there, dry heaving, Charlie is at my lap, mouth open wide, tonguing my pants a little too close to my groin. I use both hands now to shove him away. My head's a spinning mess. I look at my slime-green pants, the slime-green linoleum, walls and floor.

It's just too awful for comment when suddenly Cole pulls at the crotch of her pants, bangs on the floor with her bottle of Jack and whistles for Charlie.

That old Saint Bernard spins on his heels and tromps over to the chair. He starts lapping away between Cole's legs with that huge tongue of his, slobbering, snorting and licking.

I hang there with my mouth open. Chris is watching in a state of pure shock.

Cole just goes off into a drunken world of her own. She raises her peg legs over the arms of the easy chair, petting the horse-neck of Charlie the dog. She is getting herself a good slobbery tongueful of puppy love. The dog looks like he's had a meal or two there before and Cole's eyes are rolling in her whisky head, turning side to side, with her peg legs shaking in the air. Her big green-olive, crossed-eyed nipples are about to pop.

Chris and I look at each other. She is in heaven with her dog and doesn't give a shit what we think. We slowly walk out of the room, down the stairs and out the barn door.

We hear her moaning, swearing to the rafters and shaking the corrugated siding of the barn, and then we're long gone down the highway in a driving frenzy that lasts for days to come.

18

Urban Packs a Gun

The locals say it's the windiest day in memory.
Ayup. Good strong spring gusts howl outside, pushing a torrent of wetness across the street.

I sit on a bench in a cafe in the middle of Bar Harbor,
Maine.

Chris is off chasing down another name in the tiny
black address book. This time I bail out and save myself
the trouble. He can pick me up when he's done.

He leaves me in town and heads for the white-trash
side of Mt. Desert Island. I pass the time near the square,
shooting the breeze with locals. After two bottles of stout
and half a pizza, I meet a man named Urban.

This is not a bleak meeting, despite the bleakness of
the day.

I've just watched a woman run her car straight into a
three-foot ditch. The left front end plunged vertical,
leaving the back tires to spin in the wet air. The driver is
resigned to phone a tow truck, but a man waved her down
and says, "Just give me a second and I'll have you out of
there."

He is soon squatting under the car in his grubby pair

of pants and with one deep grunt lifts the car horizontal, commanding her to "Slap her in reverse and step her out."

She's out of there, with the rescuer brushing water off his brow.

He rambles in through the door, caked with mud from some backwoods trek, twigs and leaves clinging to his backside. Inside he bends down to cup a cat in his palm and starts to recite a poem. He adjusts the earring in his right ear and I know he's a bit queer.

He comes across like a baby faced butch, but looks like he could pack a mean right hook.

"Let's have a drink," he says, joining me on my bench. We exchange names.

He calls himself a 165-pound overgrown midget. He is a bit short, but not that short. I think he's strong, witty and wild as the storm that brews over the sea.

He sees me reading the paper and starts ranting about the bigots in town.

"If people say sexist or racist comments, I confront them. I've always stuck up for the underdog. And I'll put money where my mouth is," he tells me as we settle in to a drink.

"I've always said that I'm the outcast of the outcast. I'm, like, in the one percent of the ten percent. Basically I'm a redneck and that's hard for a lot of people to handle, especially since I'm gay."

My gaydar had already done its work well, but I smack my lips in mock surprise. Of course, he knows I'm as queer as a unicorn and buddies up to me.

Urban Hutchins is his full name and he can speak in proper English. Born, bred and harvested in Maine, he knows the backwoods of Mt. Desert like it's his own backyard.

And he is a talker. Yes he is.

Driving a full sized Ford pickup with mounted gunracks, sporting a fifth-generation carpenter's stance, and spewing a loud, gleeful laugh, he is totally male, bursting with testosterone. But I can still see some boyish charm behind his eyes.

He starts into some tough Bubbaland banter with a couple of cold running trappers who walk in the door. But then he turns the wheel back to me with intricate dialogue and English-professor enunciation.

Yeah, he walks the fence and I like him.

"I talk fast and mean, I like to hunt, fish, track, shoot, ski, camp, snorkel and wrestle—which is the only sport I've ever liked because it's about the art of balance.

"I also like to collect books, and I ask questions. Even though I didn't finish high school, that hasn't kept me from learning. I'm always picking things up, learning from other people. Sometimes it's useful, sometimes it's just talk. I particularly like the banter from these old Mainers. In Maine, the men call everything her, or she. Just slap *her* and drive...or clamp down on *her*...or don't *she* go Jesus." Urban says the words with a drawl thick as chowder.

"Last winter I was plowing through a slick dirt road and got stuck. I was dressed up, so when I found a local guy he thought I'd be some city slicker come up from the flatlands. But I just pitched right in with a shovel to show that I wasn't afraid of dirt."

"He said, 'Keep your wheel on the berm and when ya get about to that tree you want to be shovelin' the coal to her.'

"That's how they talk here. It's a heavy Acadian accent, like the Cajuns in Louisiana, only northern."

The rain dies down and Urban wants to know if I want to go shooting. He packs a pistol and likes to practice on a friend's back forty acres.

We hop in his truck. His bumper sticker reads "Homophobia Is a Social Disease" and a pink triangle is glued on the dash like a badge of honor. He shows me his pistol under the front seat, unloaded. We buckle up and he "slaps her in drive" and "shovels the coal."

"People know you're gay?" I ask, wondering how he fares in the backwoods of Maine.

"It's common knowledge around here. Almost everyone knows me by name. But I'm always prepared for Maine bigots."

We pull up a dirt road, squeal behind a farmhouse and come to a stop in the wet woods. Urban pulls out a box of bullets and a pair of ear protectors from under the seat.

The woods are dripping from the rain. We slosh through a meadow and down a path that ends in a junk-filled clearing. This is the target range. While he loads his pistol, he illustrates the protocol of using a gun.

"No doubt about it," he yells. "It's phallic as hell and it's all about power."

I give it a try and nearly knock myself to the ground. His pistol packs a punch.

"You ever have to use this?" I ask.

"No, but sometimes I've come close."

"Why? You get harassed?"

"Oh, you betcha," he says while knocking off a shot.

We're shooting at bottles on top of an old stove, and bullets are flying.

"About five years ago I was down at the Irving Maineway with a few friends to pick up some wine. It's the only twenty-four-hour convenience store in town. A dozen local jocks were holding up the wall, shootin' the breeze when I made my way inside.

"One of them says, 'How old is that kid?' when I

walked in. I knew the game and was expecting to be hustled for beer.

"Another one of them says, 'He's that tinkerbell.'

"I heard it but made no comment.

"When I went back outside I couldn't find my friends and decided to join the crowd. That's when one towering thug leaned into my face and said, 'You a tinkerbell?'

"So I said, 'I hear Tinkerbell carries a pretty big gun,' and left it at that.

"A bunch of them started in on me, like saying 'Fucking queer, who let you in town?'

"I just stood there. This is my town too. I've lived here nearly all my life and I'll be damned if a bunch of young jocks were going to scare me off.

"Someone else yelled, 'Why you wearing an earring in your right ear?'

"I saw nearly a dozen studded left ears on these guys, so I said, 'Well, I guess I'm wearing an earring on my *right* ear because I'm gay!'

"That got them going. I started to walk away when one of them said, 'That's right queer, you better run because I was about to crack open your head.'

"Well, I froze in my tracks. It was one thing to leave because things were cooling off, but to be accused of running? I don't run from anything. So I took a breath, slowly turned, pointed toward my tormentor and said, 'You might want to reconsider, because if you even try, I'll tear you apart.'

"Well, you should have seen everyone else jump out of their cars like there's going to be a fight. They were calling me every name in the book. Their leader, this guy named Rufus, was in my face and calling me a disgusting faggot.

"I looked up at this pathetic boy and said, 'The one who screams faggot loudest is usually one himself. In medical terms it's referred to as latent homosexuality.'

"That had them going. Rufus was leaning into me and about fifty people were pressed around. I just stood my ground and looked straight ahead, keeping my body braced for the worst.

"Someone yelled, 'Just hit him in the head with a crescent and be it done with.'

"That's when I finally got scared.

"Suddenly this other hot shit, named Ti, came up. He was, like, the pride of the football team. And he wants to know what's going on.

"Rufus says, 'This little queer's giving us shit!'

"Well, for the next hour I refused to leave or give up my ground. Every time they'd put me down I'd hit them with a verbal rebound.

"A lot of them started drifting back to their cars, but Rufus was still staring me down. Finally I inched out of the crowd for the phone booth and carefully dialed 911. For a second it seemed like my fate hung on whether that phone worked.

"When the operator answered I said, 'Could you puleeeease get some officers over to the Maineway immediately? I'm here being harassed and threatened with violence by a crowd of adolescent males because I'm a homosexual!'

"Twenty minutes later, officer Les was there dispersing the crowd and sending me on my way. He tells me that I can't file a police report unless it happens again. I wasn't very encouraged."

The gun is smoking from another round, but I haven't hit a single target. At least I'm not falling over from the recoil. Urban loves this, but it's starting to rain again. We pack up, get into the pickup and head back to town.

"So what became of all of that? Did they ever bother you again?" I want to know, especially since I'm now riding in his truck.

"No, not really. Except that the next day, when I went into town for breakfast, I passed Rufus on his work break outside LaVerdier's drugstore. I kept walking straight past him, just ignoring him until he said, 'Yeah, you're a real stud.'

"I was totally exasperated at having to deal with this jerk again. I turned and said, 'You talking to me?'

"He said, 'Don't you get started with me again!'

"I couldn't believe it. My blood was beginning to boil. I said, 'You are extremely ignorant and really ought to grow up. You make me very angry, little boy!' I was at that point nose to navel with Rufus.

"He said, 'You ought to see a shrink!'

"Well, I couldn't help myself and I spat at him, but missed, and then turned to continue on my way.

"Rufus took me by the shoulders, attempting to shove me, and said, 'Hey, get back here.'

"That did it. I had waited an entire lifetime for the opportunity to finally release some pent-up hostility against bigoted homophobes. Rufus stepped toward me. I whipped around, flung off my jacket and thought, *Thank you, God, for this opportunity to explain myself in terms that this little slush-brained punk can understand,* and I pounced and swung a hard right hook into his face.

"Rufus went down against the Coke machine with a thud. His buddy bolted out of the store, followed by the manager screaming at me to back off.

"But I had long since backed off. I was calmly dusting my hands and said, 'Could you be so kind as to keep your employees from shoving people around?'

"I pulled myself together, took one hard look at Rufus and walked away with a smile. That's the last time they ever bothered me."

We arrive back in town and the light of the day is fading across Frenchman's Bay. I make note to call on Urban the next time I'm faced by an angry mob.

"I'm angry," Urban says, "disappointed and impatient with this country. I feel no one should have to go through this harassment shit nor work this hard to keep a positive attitude. I'm sick of being subjected to discrimination because of my sexuality. There is no reason to have to deal with this ignorance, which is in my opinion brought about by the church, which is all about racism, sexism, discrimination, oppression, fear and living with blinders on."

I clap my hands together for Urban Hutchins and swear I'll vote for him if he ever runs for office.

Urban drops me off at the center of town. It begins to pour again. I put out my gun-weary hand and give him a firm shake. But then he jumps out and gives me a big hug and a kiss on the cheek. People stare but he doesn't care.

"What's your personal dream, Urban?" I finally ask.

"My personal dream?" Urban drums his fingers on the door of his pickup.

"I want to be the Martin Luther King of the gay community," he yells as he pulls away, his taillights blinking a friendly goodbye.

He may be. But I think more likely he'll become its Malcolm X.

19

The Mississippi Queen

Chris's eyes glow green in the light of the dash. The moon's risen but an inch over the bay and I slurp on a pickle that I got from the market.

When I get in the van I cross my legs like I'm mad from waiting. Chris is quiet, leaning forward, hunched over the wheel as we leave Bar Harbor. His pale-blue shirt is wet like he'd been swimming and his dimpled brow is bent close to the glass.

It's nearly midnight, and there's no view because the fog is hugging the road. So we're going kind of slow, keeping a wary eye out for deer.

I let out a sigh and say, "So, did you find them?" even though I know he didn't.

What he did find was another amputee of sorts. This time it was a girl about his age. She'd lost her thumb on a saber saw while cutting wood for a cupboard she had been building Helen. She hadn't seen Helen for more than a year. It was mighty strange—two out of two people in the book were missing parts of themselves. If you count Chris, that makes three.

"Sounds like a trend," I say, but am sure that Chris has already thought of this.

"It's a cult and we're getting out of here," Chris moans. "Everyone that Helen comes near meets an accident."

My thoughts exactly, and I wonder where we're going. "You still going to take me to Portland? And I'm talking about Oregon."

He's nodding his head but says, "How about a stop in Memphis first?"

It doesn't take me more than one guess to know that the next name in the address book probably lives there. That little old book with its five names has plenty to answer for. No amount of talk will change his mind.

Memphis is a town that has spelled trouble for me since the days I lived there. I tell him about the time my mom took me and my brother to Graceland. We waited half the day hoping to see a glimpse of the King. Then she shut her finger in the car door. We never did see Elvis.

I start talking about Memphis like it's an old friend of mine. Paddleboats churning down the river, Cotton Parades and streets full of blues seem like a dream. Next thing I know I'm feeling kind of nostalgic. I want to catch a glimpse of the old Mississippi. Before I can even change my mind, he takes me up on my word.

We're on our way to the land of cotton.

As we cruise through the night, time feels like a tunnel swallowing us whole. The thick white air rolls across the highway, playing games with the light. Bumps the size of melons on the road make for a rickety ride. Chris checks his clock, a little number glued to the dash, and sets the time for Tennessee.

We may be fifteen hundred miles away, but he's already there in his scrambling mind. He drives fast, like he's running from the law. I slump out of my seat and crawl into the back, leaving the driving to him.

Twelve hours later we're barreling down the Blue Ridge Parkway. It's noon on Wednesday and the Appalachian Trail snakes along the southwestern crest. We make a pit stop for fuel and Chris looks wide-eyed like a startled bull. Something's going on and I can feel him shaking. His fingers drum on the steering wheel fast as a horse once we're back on the road.

"We're not stopping till we get there," he says.

"You're not okay, are you?" I ask after a few miles.

His face is red and his eyes bulge like a catfish.

"Sometimes I get heat flashes. I feel hot, like I'm going to explode, or my body's on fire and there's no way to cool down."

I touch his head, carefully, and feel that he's burning hot. You could bake a casserole on the back of his neck, it's so wicked warm.

"You coming down with a bug?" I say, rolling down my window for some fresh air.

"No. It'll pass. It's all in my groin."

"What do you mean?"

"I mean, I can't have sex, you know. And it sort of builds up. Like I can't get relief."

I ponder this for a while. That would make him sort of like a monk, although the unintentional kind.

"There's no way around it? I mean, isn't there something you can do?"

He's not answering and I don't ask more.

I sit back and let Chris cruise up the highway when I

finally notice a knife. It sits in the little cubbyhole below the dash. It's been sitting there all along. This worries me a bit. I finally ask him what it's doing there.

Well, it's the goddamn kitchen knife. The one he used to do the deed.

He scares me for a second when he yells, "Don't touch it!"

I pick it up anyway. It's a plain serrated kitchen knife—good for cutting tomatoes or a loaf of bread.

"Man, what are you doing with this? Are you nuts?" I yell.

"I don't know. I hung on to it after El Paso. Just hasn't been the right time to toss it yet."

This is too sick for me and I toss it out the window without a blink.

He totally freaks. He slams on the brakes. I think for a second he's going to run us off the road. I'm holding on to the dash, with my feet to the floor.

"Why the hell did you do that?" he screams.

"I just did you a favor. It's done now and over with. Let go of that knife. You don't need it. You shouldn't have it. And if that's the only good thing I can do for you, then so be it. What were you going to do with it anyhow, kill someone?"

"Maybe!"

"Who?"

"Maybe me."

My God. A suicidal eunuch and I'm probably his only friend. We're stopped now in the middle of the road, the other cars streaming by. I think about getting out and just bidding a friendly goodbye. His twisted life hovers on a precipice and seems an inch short of falling over.

He breathes hard at the wheel while the heat streams

sweat from his head. A crippled heartbeat of a moment goes by. I close my eyes and smell the fumes from the road. The corners of my mouth are tight as I start to open the door.

He says, "Get it!"

I say, "No."

And then in a moment of truth I say, "The knife is not your friend. I am. So choose between us."

The four feet separating us are full of thought balanced on a sharp edge. Even if half a million cars go by, I will wait at the door until he makes up his mind, because my heart is with helping my friend.

He sits poised in a rage, ready to pounce. Yet as the seconds tick by on his little clock, and as the traffic skirts around us, his face slowly comes apart.

Not that many cars go by before he begins to cry.

Giant heaves run up his back and shake his neck. He lets the river flow from his rattled soul into his lap and down to the floor. No dam in the world could hold back this sorrow.

And I just wait.

After he finally forces out his last tear, his face puffy and red, he takes no time making his choice. If a friend is all he needs to keep his life moving on, then I, for what it's worth, step into that role. He takes me by the hand and pulls me back in.

The wheels spin forward and our journey resumes. Our shirts are off, on the floor, soaked with sweat. Our arms fly out the windows, dancing in the wind, and we travel in silence with our hands held.

We drive through the night and into another day. The fast food meccas off the interstate are our only friends as we head to Tennessee.

On Thursday afternoon we arrive in Memphis. Our home at the end of this road is a sleazy motel on Poplar Avenue.

And his knife remains far behind.

Noon again and another day. I crack open an eye. I'm lying facedown on a bed with my clothes and shoes on. I hate that. It's like never really going to sleep.

Humidity hangs over the room now that we've reached the South. Traffic bellows on the street. I start to think I'm lying near a creek with fish splashing upstream, but it's only water running in a tub. I look toward the sliver under the bathroom door and jerk my head up quick. I see water seeping across the room.

"Chris?" I holler.

He's not in bed and his clothes are draped over the TV. I can hear a steady splash and a low moan.

"Chris!" I yell again.

I pull myself out of bed. The water's a good half inch deep and headed out the front door. It follows a path around the bed like it's done this before.

I don't bother to knock at the bathroom door. A faceful of steam hits me and I see him lying in the tub in an odd sort of way.

My heart jumps. I think he's drowned.

His face is under water with only his nose jutting out, sucking in air. His eyes are closed and his cheeks puff out. His legs are straddling the faucet. And there it is, under the force of water, sticking up.

I look.

His toes twitch in the air as the rush of water swirls across his penis. I guess this is as good as it gets, because there's not much to grab hold of.

He's turning his head side to side, moaning like a calf, when he opens his right eye and sees me.

His head snaps up and his legs fold toward him, sloshing more water on the floor.

"What do you want?" He pulls himself into the tub looking very betrayed.

"For God's sake Chris, the tub is overflowing. It's running out the door."

He jumps up, eyes wide, and sees me standing in the flood. Then he lunges for the taps and shuts them off.

All is quiet.

I swallow nervously, embarrassed for both of us.

He stands there, dripping wet, and looks guiltily down.

"Sorry," he says.

"Hey, *I'm* sorry. I didn't mean to barge in."

"I'm sorry you had to see."

My tongue twists in a circle while the water drains out the door. "Oh, come on. You think I'm bothered?"

"Now you know how pathetic I am." He's truly ashamed.

"Oh for Christ's sake. You think sitting under a faucet like that is pathetic? Look Chris, even Annie Sprinkle recommends using a bathtub if a waterfall can't be found."

Chris laughs. I reach for an armful of towels and start mopping up the mess in the bedroom.

He steps out of the tub and helps me soak up the water from the shag carpeting.

"So, does it work?" I say.

"Fuck, nothing works. I've tried everything. You know, it's like I can't even come close. Sometimes I think I'm almost there, but then it gives out. I've used vibrators, penis pumps, aphrodisiacs…nothing helps. What would you do?"

"What would I do?" I stare at the wall. "I don't really know what to tell you, Chris. If it were me, I'd probably hope to find a lover. Someone with a lot of patience. Someone who you felt strongly attracted to."

"What about you?"

"Yeah, what about me?" I nervously smile. "I'm not so sure."

"Why, aren't you attracted to me?"

"Yes, I'm attracted to you! But are you really attracted to me?"

"I don't know. Maybe we should just try it."

I look at Chris standing there, dripping wet, nervous, naked, raw and exposed.

"The truth is, it would just take time getting used to the way you are. You know, your injury. Plus, you've never done it with a man. I'm not so sure it's what you want."

"You're right," he says. "I'm not so sure a man *is* what I want. It's women I think of. But maybe I should try it with you."

"Not yet, Chris. Let's give it time."

And we continue mopping up the floor.

The third name in the address book lives in Germantown. That afternoon I stay behind at the motel.

Chris walks out like a new man. His eyes are clear. He's in a good mood because he got word that Claudia had been in town only a month before.

I don't think much of this and keep my mouth shut. Like, what does he think he'll find?

At dusk, before the sun sinks below the Mississippi, I take a long-awaited stroll. It's been years since I walked these streets. Back in the days when "coloreds" and "whites" were not supposed to mix. Back in the days when Woolworth's was swank and a penny could buy you a lot— if you were a kid, that is.

I walk with long strides through town to the Peabody Hotel, north of Beale. The hotel ducks aren't in their duckpond today, so I take the elevator to the roof and look around.

Over by the river is a carnival with a big tall Ferris wheel and lots of little rides. From up high it looks like a cardboard maze, a tinsel town peppered with pretty marbles.

I go back down the elevator and skip the few blocks to the water. The Mississippi is not a pretty river. Sort of mean and brown. The banks aren't filled out and green yet. And the trees look withered and old. But still, it's mighty in size, deep enough for big barges and wide enough to make for a scary swim.

I don't plan to swim.

North of the bridge sits the Pyramid. Old King Tut would turn in his tomb if he had half a notion of what they do below these walls.

I walk through the entrance of the carnival, paying five dollars to get in. Trash blows in the strong breeze from downriver. The rides whir mechanically under flashing neon signs. Hordes of kids wait for the Scramble and the Pirate Ship.

Screams pierce the river walk and I look for the midway. Sawdust carpets the floor and a million colored lights blink in patterns down the column of game booths. The Penny Toss now costs a dime and the Ring Toss gets you a tiny stuffed bear.

I stop at a pink-and-white candy-striped cart on big wheels. A lady works inside, busy popping corn. She hands me a big bag and I give her a buck. I notice her hands are sort of large. Not like a mother's, worn big from slapping kids, but just big-boned.

Her hair is a little bit off. I look close and see she's wearing a wig. It sits slightly askew. Her nails are well manicured. She laughs good and loud when I tip her an extra quarter for the real butter on top.

I'm standing outside the booth when another girl comes around to relieve the first. The woman inside comes out the door and takes off her apron. *Oh, lordy.* She's bigger than I first thought. I don't mean fat. I mean tall, with wide shoulders broad enough for a linebacker. Her legs would support a good-sized man.

"What are you looking at?" she says.

She stands there in her pink dress with white bobby socks and black-and-white shoes. Her black skin looks even blacker against the pink.

"I said, what are you looking at, honey?" she asks again.

Her voice has a warm nasal tone that catches between the vowels.

"Wow. You're tall," I say looking up, and I'm six feet two.

"That's because I'm a big-boned girl," she says. "And my momma was a big-boned girl, too!"

"She was as big as you?"

"Well, not as big as me," her voice cracks in a laugh. "I'm manufactured."

"Manufactured?" I like the concept but don't understand the context. "What do you mean?"

She looks around the crowd and leans down to whisper low in my ear. "I used to be a boy."

I look again. Now the legs make sense. I wonder if she ever played football and ask her name.

"Samantha," she chuckles. "But you can just call me the Mississippi Queen."

I like her.

When she hears I'm a tourist she wants to show me around, so we set out for town. We stop at the ladies' room, where a quarter-mile line of Memphis belles are waiting for a stall. She walks in past them all and takes her sweet time redressing herself.

She comes out wearing platform shoes, a white jumpsuit with silver buttons and another wig. Samantha pushes seven feet now, with a big voice and hefty smile that could sweep a crowd off its feet.

People twist their necks to watch. She wiggles while she walks. And she is a queen.

"How long you lived here?" I ask.

"I was born here and I'm going to die here."

"How do you know you're going to die here?"

"I have AIDS, that's why."

I'm sorry to hear it and I say so.

"Don't be sorry, just stay safe. Hey, do you like my new shoes?" Her moonwalking shoes have big ugly straps that buckle her in.

I nod my head. Not exactly what I'd wear to the prom.

We walk by a group of sailors, and Samantha breaks off, cruising one for a moment too long. He calls her a whore and throws a Coke bottle over her head.

"Asshole!" She turns, walking back with me. "Sailors

aren't fun anymore. I used to clean up here with the boys
in white. Now they're nothing but Republican farm boys
with corn cobs up their asses, if you ask me."

"So, you lived here your whole life?"

"No, I've lived everywhere. I've lived in San Francisco, L.A., Paris, Moscow, Hong Kong."

Somehow I don't believe this.

"How long have you been a drag queen?"

She stops me in my tracks.

"Honey, I am *not* a drag queen. I am a woman. Or a
transgendered woman. You can take your pick."

"So are you, uh, do you have, uh..."

"Do I have a pussy? Is that what you're trying to ask?
Yes, I am anatomically correct now," she says with a big
smile. "It's been six months. I saved every penny of mine
for over ten years for this. When I got diagnosed with
AIDS, everyone just said to give it up. Like, why waste all
of that money on something that won't do me much good
when I'm dead?

"Well, I said, if they're going to bury me anytime
soon, they're going to bury me a woman. I mean a
manufactured woman, if you know what I mean.

"Eight years ago I bought lots of work clothes with my
charge card. I must have charged a thousand dollars, easy.
I was working at the hospital as a registered nurse."

"How come you're working at the carnival?" I ask.

"For the extra money. Plus, I got canned at the
hospital."

"How come?"

"Oh, you know. I liked to make the patients feel extra
good, especially in the terminal ward. They loved me
there."

"Are you talking sex?"

"No, I'm talking genital stimulation. I have a special massage."

"You were doing it to patients?"

"Only if they wanted it."

"What, you would masturbate them?"

Samantha rolled her eyes.

"You're a true Florence Nightingale."

"Yeah, well anyhow I'd bought this entire wardrobe for work years ago and started dressing the part. My supervisor threw a fit. She called me on it and things got tough for a while, honey. They had me go before the goddamn hospital board. Well, not me, but my case. It was to see if I should be allowed to dress at work even though I was pre-op.

"Well, they ruled against me and said that as long as I was an anatomical boy, I couldn't wear women's clothes to work. So I had to put my clothes in storage. I could still step out at night."

"So what happened?"

"I was a man right up to the very end. I had my boobs done, electrolysis, my hair, my beard, and my voice was already there. But as long as I had a little wee-wee they still made me dress like a man. Honey, if I was them, I would have seen the light. I was causing more of a ruckus that way than if I had come to work in my nurse's frock. I mean, my titties are good-sized, don't you think?"

They *were* good-sized.

"I went overseas to have the finishing touches last year. Well, when I came back I was at work within two months. Oh you should of seen her go."

"Who?"

"Me, that's who. So I walked in and I was a brand-new *woman*. I had makeup and rings and heels. Their jaws just dropped. I changed my name tag that day to Samantha, you know, like on *Bewitched?*"

I knew. But this wasn't the Samantha I'd known.

"When I pulled out my box of work clothes that I'd stored for six years, nothing fit. Guess that tells you what hormones will do for you. I used to be thin like you. So I was down to two basics sets. I'd spent all my money and couldn't afford any more.

"But then they fired my ass. That's why I'm working down here at the carnival, picking up a little change. Never know when I'm going to go down."

"Down where?" I ask.

"To the grave, honey."

Samantha walks around town with me on her arm. Crowds part for us and I feel like we're working the street even though I'm not.

"Were you always a nurse?"

"Not always an RN, but I've always been nursing," she cackles.

"Like, what were you nursing?"

"Boys. You know. On the street."

"Sex?"

"Yes."

"Here in Memphis?"

"Yes."

"I thought you'd lived all over."

"I lied," she says and lets out a big donkey laugh.

Three shades past eleven and the air is still warm. The streets buckle with bourbon and the music soars. The bars are hopping. We walk into the back room of a sleazy pit of a lounge she calls home at night. And she is working it, making back-room deals in the men's restroom.

After half an hour she joins me at my table.

"What about AIDS?" I ask.

"Honey, I'm strictly hand jobs with rubber gloves. I give them all that special glow. Anything for the cause," she winks.

At midnight I tell her about Chris.

Samantha gets excited and begs for the challenge. "Honey I've done the best of them. I've brought life to where they'd long since nailed the coffin closed. I'm talking quadriplegics, paraplegics, amputees, terminal cases...everything up to brain dead. I can do them all."

"You think you could do a penis amputee?"

She nods her head. "I'd even do it for free."

At two in the morning Samantha and I quietly enter the motel room. Chris is lying there with his wide bull eyes heating up again. He's fried and barely fit for words when I introduce him to Samantha.

We all three hang in the middle of the room with its white textured speckles on the ceiling and riverboat papered walls. The mismatched lamps are a decade apart in age and the one crooked chair has a short leg.

I notice these things while Chris lies in a white T-shirt and nothing else on the bed. There are big, cup-sized circles under his eyes and his arms wrap around me like a wounded bird.

"What should I do?" he asks.

"I brought you a nurse. Why don't you give her a try."

He leans up against the headboard while I sit down at his side.

Samantha pulls out her gloves and we all stare eye to eye.

I wait.

He wonders.

I look.

He finally nods.

I walk over to the TV and turn it on. I do a channel surf until I find an old *I Love Lucy* rerun and glue my eyes to the screen.

In a dark corner, they pull off their clothes and throw them on the floor. For the next few hours Samantha's magic hands do their professional work.

And the man without a penis finally gets laid.

20

Heat Wave in Little Rock

I am done with Memphis. Memphis is done with me. The way I know these things is when my feet start to itch.

Chris and Samantha are bound together like two rabbits in a hole. Can't tear them apart for days. He's got the money, she's got the talent, and together they have themselves a perfect little world, which leaves me out in the cold.

I feel kind of sad but relieved. Chris and I didn't get far, but we got where he needed to be. He says he's going to stay awhile. He's found what he was looking for. Now it's my turn to move on.

I tell Chris on a Monday that today's the day. Doesn't do me much good to stay sad-eyed and sleeping by myself like the third wheel I am. I pack up my bag.

Chris and Samantha drive me to the bus. I wonder how I let myself ever get attached to this man. He kisses me wetly like a kiwi, a little rough on the edge. He says they'll both come looking for me someday, but I don't count on it.

Samantha squeezes my hand and gives me a rib-cracking hug.

They think they're in love, and I might be inclined to agree. I board the bus for Arkansas and wave goodbye to the unlikely pair.

Two hours on an easy roll across the delta, looking out at cotton fields, and I am the only white man on board. I'm taking the Greyhound to Little Rock, where I'll make a change. Two seats away sit two black women arm in arm. I like the closeness between them. I can feel the heat of their bodies and smell the sweat under their arms.

One of them holds a pack of Kents in her hand, very ladylike, but doesn't light one up. She sits square-shouldered, her head back against the seat. Her friend is doing crossword puzzles on her knees.

Their faces are warm and friendly. I bet they're close to fifty, with a grandkid or two each.

"God I want a cigarette," the bigger one says. Her legs rock back and forth.

"How you supposed to quit smoking if you keep them around?"

"Oh, shut up."

"What's a prairie dog, six letters, starts with a 'c'?"

"Coyote," the other says, and she howls in her hand, imitating the sound.

The bus roars down the highway. The blue Ozark hills aren't far away. I was born a hundred miles away from here, in Mountain Home, about the year the lake was made. My daddy helped build the Bull Shoals Dam across the river. And my head was kissed by former President Herbert Hoover at the dedication ceremony. Maybe that's why I lost all my hair and dream of being president some day.

The older I get, the more distance I feel from this land of my birth. The images I carry in my mind are of nature, old folks, slow-moving rivers and people who still say "Hi" whenever they get the chance. I could always trust that time would stand still and the friendly people of the Ozarks would always be there with their doors open.

Unless you're a queer.

Now it seems the same as everywhere else. People know you're queer and slam the door in your face. Except my family. But that's a blood thing and those ties are still strong.

My grandma, now she was the most interesting person I think I've ever known. Since I was a little kid I could hardly believe I was her grandson. And I couldn't understand why she'd never sit still. Whether churning butter, fueling her cookstove with kindling, wringing wet clothes on the wringer, canning green beans; she was always doing something. I loved to watch the way she moved. She was as graceful as a person could be. Moved kind of slow, but her hands seemed to know without her looking where everything in the house was. I even bet she could find her way around blind without trying.

Whenever I'd come visit, she was the one who captivated my attention. I'd just as soon lean through the kitchen window and watch her whip up another batch of biscuits and gravy than go down to the barn to feed the hogs.

But she's dead and gone.

And she would be having a fit to sit with this busload of dark-skinned people. Her prejudice never softened.

My dad was a fine man. He was always back to tuck us in late at night and gone by the early sun, digging deep holes in the ground, mining for ore.

But he's gone, too. Buried alive in the mine.

I think of sneaking through the Ozarks without saying a peep to my family. Just sort of lurking on by like a transient breezing through town.

I always did want to spy on my home. I could watch my family from afar, see them doing their routines without knowing I'm in town, without rolling out their red carpet and making everything nice.

What do they really do when I'm not around? Is the house all a big mess and the toilets backed up? Are they talking bad about me when I'm far from earshot? For a moment I consider spending a couple of days on my silent mission.

But I don't. I'll come back home when it's Christmas and snow's on the ground. I'll see the family when everyone's feeling special and the turkey's on the stove. That's when I'll come.

We unload at the Little Rock station and it's hot as hell. That's double the trouble in the sticky air. One humid slap across the brow and I'm already wanting the air-conditioned bus. But I've got three hours to kill.

The whole state, I learn, is sitting out a late-spring heat wave. The sizzling sun in Little Rock has everyone looking for shade. It's only eleven in the morning and already the mercury is past the ninety-five-degree mark, with humidity so thick you need a tarp to keep it off you.

I head for shade down by a pavilion on the Arkansas River, picking up six bean-and-cheese Taco Bell burritos along the way. A disproportionate number of Buicks command all the parking spaces. Searching for even the slightest breeze, I wander into a small field, taking up a seat under a sprawling tree. As I wipe my brow, a blast of water from above hits my neck.

"What the hell?" I look up.

Two young rednecks are perched up in the tree, blasting me with megasized water guns. They sit fifteen feet overhead, sweating like steamed corn, their 501s hugging their blistering balls. They continue to pump their guns, but the water feels good.

"OK, wiseasses," I say flinging off my shirt and exposing my back. "As long as you're at it, wet me down all the way!"

"No way, faggot!" the shorter of the two yells as he cuts loose another blast at my left ear.

I stand to face the guys, wondering aloud how total strangers could so easily figure out my sexual status. Just as I prepare to deliver a verbal defense against mindless name calling, another blast hits me.

"You cheap fucks," I cry. "Cut the crap."

They laugh. But suddenly one of the tree-dwelling homophobes screams "Snake!" I look to my left, and there indeed is a good-sized snake making its way around the trunk.

I run like lightning back toward the pavilion, where groups of lunchtime workers are having their break. I hear two women snickering and turn around. It's the same two from the bus, sitting on a bench, quietly surveying the scene. They share a parasol. They've hiked their dresses up past their knees, hoping to catch a breeze.

They eye me laughingly and say hello.

"I heard what they called you," the bigger one of the two says in a smoky voice. I half expect a sodomy sermon to ensue, and I turn toward the parking lot.

"You know what I'd do?" her partner spoke in an even lower voice.

I began to walk. *First water guns, now fire and brimstone,* I think to myself.

"I'd bugger the bastards till they scream for mercy."
she said.

Then they both cackle, deep-throated rasps that roll
across the lawn.

I stop cold in my tracks. "Excuse me?" I say, turning
to face them.

"You heard me," the second one snickers. "I'd bugger
'em. That's what they want."

My eyes widen and I scratch my head. "You mean,
like..."

"You know just what I mean," she says with a devilish
grin. "We'll hold 'em down."

I gawk in amazement, trying to imagine this imposs-
ible scene of two older black women restraining two rowdy
rednecks while I did the deed! I notice my new friends
wear identical rings and are obviously close. Probably the
only little old lesbian black mamas in the Ozarks.

"I'd toss them the snake," the first one says. "It's not
poisonous, but it'll give them a scare they won't forget.
There's no laws against that." Her brows arch at her friend.
"Maybe they'll pass out from fright, and you can proceed
with plan A." They burst out in another loud, wet laugh.

I wink and head back toward the tree. The guys are
still up there, eyeing the snake and looking at me. I walk
under them and retrieve my shirt. Doesn't take long
before I am under fire again in a barrage of water.

But now I do as I was told.

Not the buggery, but the snake tossing. I lob the six-
foot snake up in the tree and the rednecks scream for
their lives. They scramble down the branches while the
dykes roar with laughter in the summer heat.

I guess that's how to pass the time in the Natural State.

21

Big Al and the Hand of God

At two in the afternoon the bus fills up to the rails, and I'm feeling beat. Can't say much for this traveling alone in a world of homophobes. It's going to be a hell of a long way back to Portland.

I was first in line. For a change I'm sitting at the very front, where the chatty old women usually sit, diagonal from the driver and with a front-row view. Evil-eyed, wrinkled ladies file past me, mad as hell that I'm taking The Spot.

I move to the window, making room for one more, but I bet no one will sit next to me. I suspect it's a warning they print on the tickets: DO NOT SIT BY TALL BALD STRANGERS WITH WILD LOOKS IN THEIR EYES.

No one sits next to me and I'm glad.

The road to Oklahoma City is full of miniature craters. The dirty dog is rocking and a rolling through the hills. Big old tractor-trailers whizz on by as I wave Arkansas a curt farewell with a blink of my eyes.

About eight P.M. we pull into Oklahoma City to change buses and eat.

Leather-skinned ladies clutching Bibles are waiting in

line at the KFC. In front of me stands a family that looks
Cherokee. Their faces are round and full with big brown
eyes blinking in the florescent light. It's a mom and a pop
with four big kids holding ragged suitcases. The smallest
one stands waist-high and is rolling a yo-yo.

They order a large bucket of chicken nuggets and
share big mugs of Dr. Pepper. The mom doesn't eat but
squirts little bitty tubes of ketchup into her mouth. Guess
she likes the red.

I'm but a booth away and sit looking at their blue
black hair, thick and smooth. I ask where they're going.

"We're going to the pow wow in Gallup," the father of
the bunch says.

"You're taking the bus?"

"Yeah, lots of us are."

I look around the KFC and see more reddish faces. I
like what I see. I always did want to ride a bus full of *real*
Americans, the native kind.

We finish our meals just in time to board the bus.

This time it's already full, with nowhere to sit, including the back. I spot a single seat midway down, by a
cherry-faced woman with a crooked smile. We settle in for
the long dark road ahead.

Five black faces and my one white face are the only
non-Indian ones on board. It's not a quiet ride. The
Indians are, to say the least, a rowdy and riotous bunch.

Teenaged boys sit far at the back, throwing spitballs
and paper wads. Families laugh and talk together across
the aisles and everyone seems to know one another. They
smile and they joke, and gales of laughter roll up and
down the bus.

The woman next to me, Sue, pulls out a thick cotton
dress from her bag. She begins sewing on beads and shiny

sequins with a long needle. Rows of tassels sit on her lap. She shows me her work.

"Everyone's got several costumes," she says, "because we're all going to dance."

"They don't look very authentic," I stupidly say. "I mean, sequins and rhinestones, did they have them back then?"

"Who said we have to be authentic? This is the nineties—I use whatever I want to make a beautiful dress," she says with a soft jab in my ribs and a friendly wink.

I look around and see other hands busy tying knots and pulling thread through beads.

"Does everyone sew?"

"Yes, the men, too. Women's lib, you know."

Old women are clucking like parrots and roly-poly dads lean out into the aisle, swapping tales. It's the liveliest bus ride I've ever been on. And sleep never comes.

About the time we hit the Texas state line, the volume of sounds climbs a couple more notches. The driver hums on steadily without a word of protest. He's outnumbered anyhow.

A high-octave voice starts singing from the back. Soon the whole bus is chanting songs, which everyone seems to know. Some clap their hands and drum on their knees.

I sing along, faking the words.

"What tribe are you from?" my companion asks.

I am part Cherokee and say so. That is, if you count four generations back on my father's side. Rumor had it that my great-great-grandfather was a Cherokee chieftain. At least that's what we always wanted to believe.

Soon the word spreads and everyone's craning their necks to take a look at me. The shape of my nose becomes a focal point for comment. My nose has the right sort of hook but is not flat enough on the end.

"Looks a little too white," says the old man behind me.

My neighbors are comparing their noses to mine.

Sue takes her finger and flattens out the tip of my nose and says, "Now you're there."

She digs for a roll of Scotch tape and plaster down my nose good and flat. "That's it."

Everyone howls. I've got the Cherokee nose and the forehead, too. They launch into a low chant, welcoming me to the tribe. I chant right along like I'm really part of it. Faces rock with laughter up and down the aisle and I'm the joke for miles to come.

It's four in the morning when we hit Amarillo. Only a few of us have nodded off. Don't know what drug they're on, but there's not a drooping eye among them. Downtown is quiet like a church. Big tumbleweeds blow down the street next to the station. The smokers file out for a ten-minute break.

In the parking lot between buses men start dancing in a line, practicing for the powwow. A cool gust of night air sweeps across the plains and I want to join in the scene. It's a disco full of Indian chiefs. The women circle around, clapping their hands. The old voices rise and fall, with younger higher curlicues twisting in the air.

I stand next to Sue.

"So, where you all live?" I ask.

"Oklahoma. But some live on the road." She points to a man in a tall hat wearing a green windbreaker. "His name's Al. We call him Big Al. He lives on the road all the time. All he does is the powwow circuit."

I look at Big Al. He's tall and thin with big cheekbones sharper than a shovel's edge. His face is full of frowns. He's at the side of the circle, with two cigarettes lit in his mouth, getting double the puff. He's banging on a small stick and has the loudest voice in the crowd.

"He's Hopi," she says, setting him apart. "He's a true gypsy."

I walk over to Big Al.

Big Al doesn't look too friendly at me. He turns away and walks into the bus, where we all reload for the rest of the ride.

Twelve hard hours later the bus arrives in Gallup.

I get off and decide to stay awhile.

Gallup is a dusty town. It sits high up, amid big sharp hills, with yellow dirt and scrubbed-bare rocks everywhere. The afternoon sun burns high-altitude hot, sizzling my freckled white skin.

It's dry here. My nose cracks inside, jagged and crusty. My face feels tight and I am in need of a drink—of water, that is.

Well there's lots of drinking here, of the hundred-proof kind.

I walk through a town of bars and tacky tourist shops, Indian schlock gone wild. All around town is the Pueblo motif, tepee signs and full-feather tunics for tourists like me.

Traffic heads to the fairgrounds for the powwow, and I follow along on the wide, rutted roads. Cars and trucks park in a semicircle. And thousands more people arrive near dusk. This is the first day.

Circular camps of white canvas teepees fill the center of the grounds. Eighteen-foot-high poles stick up to the sky with banners fluttering at their tops.

Clans make claims on individual sites. Lawnchairs and barbecue grills are set up like it's a day at the beach.

Walkmans, CD players, ice coolers, propane stoves, down sleeping bags....I somehow thought this would look like a scene from the past, but it's as modern-American as the Superbowl.

I make myself a camp out toward the ring of cars. I draw a little dirt circle in the sand and put my bag down. I don't have a tent, blankets or sleeping bag. But I know this will do.

About sunset, the grand circle is called.

Excitement grows. Out come the costumes. Long, beaded dresses, short, tasseled shirts and fringed woven shawls. Feathers the color of neon rainbows flutter across heads. Dozens of tribes assemble in their costumed best and the ceremonial dances begin.

The sun hits the horizon and ribbons of gold light and shadow cover the fairgrounds. Drum circles from each tribe begin pounding out their rhythms. The drummers fall into a steady beat and cry out desert howls. I could hear the ancient voice of their people rising from their throats.

Dust rises from the stamping of many feet. Little kids in turquoise and frizzy feathered hats bounce about, their bells chiming in the air.

This is when I see Big Al.

Big Al wears a long tunic sewed in bright orange stitching with lavender beads. His long black braids are twisted around his head, which is haloed by porcupine quills. And tall white plumes dance over his back along a tassel of animal tails.

What a queen! I think to myself.

The best drag artist in town couldn't compete with this. He is dark-eyed and beautiful and has his look down. His nimble feet dance across the earth in soft moccasins.

Halfway around the circle, Big Al sees me looking at him. He turns away, scowling. I don't think he likes me and I wonder why.

Around midnight I walk over to a big open-air lodge.

Again I see Big Al. He walks in, sits down in front and talks with friends.

From the back Big Al looks like a long-haired heavy-metal dude. He seems young. He wears round hoop earrings in both ears. He's out of his feathers and wearing jogging shorts and no underwear. His legs are smooth as wax, hard-muscled and lean. When he turns, he catches me staring at him.

The sun starts to rise but no one seems tired.

Big Al jumps up and takes big long strides to a water fountain. I act sort of clumsy and stick close behind.

He finishes his drink. Big Al isn't so big from close up.

We stand there a second too long. He starts to walk away, looking down at his feet, when I say, "How long does this go on?"

He looks startled to hear me speak.

He answers me in a dusty desert voice. "Could go for days."

I hold out my hand and say my name. He looks at me hard and waits another moment too long. My hand starts to drop, but then he grabs it and shakes it roughly, nearly cracking my bones.

He holds back from speaking a word. I guess my being one sixteenth Cherokee doesn't make us brothers. Finally he says his name as sweat begins to stick between our hands, which make a big old squishy sound when we pull them apart. We both laugh at the noise.

"Like a frog walking through mud," he says.

He doesn't want to talk anymore but I know he is gay.
My gaydar is going off loud and strong. I watch him sit
down at his spot on the ground. I note the movement of
his hands and the curl of his feet. And I nod my head
when I see him whisper to a friend.

Then morning arrives.

I climb a hill. I take out a few clothes, spread them on
the dirt and lie down on them. I dig a place for my hips
and fall into a deep sleep as the low round drums beat
below.

A big old gob of wetness drops on my face and startles
me awake half the day later. There are a small puddles on
the ground. The sky's overcast with big, lightning-produc-
ing black cumulonimbus clouds. They stack up like gray
whipped cream on a cake. The sun is still shining over the
valley, but rain's about to dump very soon.

I stand up and can see for forever and a day.

Long crackles of bright lightning streak sideways
across the electrified air. I don't even think about running. I just stand on a rock, watching the whole thing.

Down below in the camp I see people running,
taking things inside. Thunder bellows across the valley
and the bolts crack even stronger. The wind is rising fast.

More people run into the lodge, where the game still
continues. I see vendors drawing tarps over their goods.
Dancers press under the awning, yet the drums never
stop.

An electrochemical bolt splinters on the earth, snapping like a dozen whips on a metal drum. I like the sound.
I live for fire. There are a million cells of light in the sky,
like the nerve endings of God. Coils of white send shivers
up my spine.

I decide to make for the camp. I head for a concrete restroom at the far edge of the grounds. No one's parked nearby and it's got a phone near the door.

Suddenly, ten steps away, I hear a big frizzled splat and a frightening hissing comes down the side of my head. A bolt of lightning from the darkened sky hits my shoulder and out my left hand. A sizzle of sparks race across my arm.

"I'm hit!" I cry

I count the seconds in slow motion.

My body feels like a five-ton rock splitting in two. The earth feels soft, with a rolling wave to it. The bottom drops out and my feet fly up. One moment up, the next moment down. I'm in a roller coaster plunging straight for hell.

My head sings, the sounds are sharp, and then my heart disappears into my feet.

"Whoa!" I scream as I hit the earth.

I see dark tunnels and pinpoints of light. Floods of buzzing madness in my head. And the full-color screen in front of my eyes goes instantly to gray and then to black.

No tunnels of light. No angelic choirs. Just a big white electric room full of clanging sounds and fluttering pops.

Then there is quiet.

And quiet.

"Jesus. You okay?" I hear a voice coming through.

I've been out but a minute when I begin opening my eyes.

The world is moving in circles. My body feels like it's been beaten up in a gang fight. I'm on the dirt and more bolts are coming down.

A teenaged girl who spoke to me is afraid to step out from the restroom door, but she pulls me in by the legs.

I feel heavier than the moon. The ground moves like an earthquake under my crawling skin as she pulls me in. We sit there alone in the little alcove.

"Jesus, it came right out your arm. I saw it," she says.

I nod. She might have seen it, but I can feel it—a mighty strong bolt of God's holy power coursing through my veins.

"Are you all right?" She sits at my side.

I don't know if I'm all right. We feel for my heart. It's beating hard. We check for my breath. It's deep and rhythmic.

"Am I alive?"

"Yeah, you're breathing."

She looks in my eyes, kind of dazed.

"Want to get to the hospital?" she's asking.

"Hospital?" I hate hospitals and that's the wrong word for me. I'm worse than an old man. I shake my head and she wants to know why.

"Costs money. Anyhow, I'm breathing and my heart's going. I guess I'm okay."

"You want me to walk you back to camp?"

"No, I'll just hang out here for a while."

She's a scared fourteen-year-old and wants her mom and dad. I nod like it's all okay and she runs off. I drag myself into the door marked MEN and lie down on the concrete floor. I can hear thunder crackling in the distance and big golf-ball-sized drops of rain are falling. I feel like I'm on a swing or floating in the sea.

The ground moves, rocking me to sleep—to a deep, deep sleep.

Twenty-four hours later, in the desert heat, I'm swatting flies off my face in the concrete room. I've wakened in a sweat. I don't have a clue where I am. The room feels kind of small. I can hear desert birds chirping in the air.

Finally it all starts coming back.

I stand up on my wobbly legs and swing through the door into the bright sunlight. I think I might be dead.

Every step I take is heavy. My legs rake across the ground one slow step at a time. I use my hands to push my thighs to get me moving along.

Outside, in the sun, there's no one around.

The farther I walk the more dead I feel.

I start to panic. I just know I'm a ghost, not really here. My vision goes double and I'm shaking like a leaf.

Finally I see a man sitting on a hill. I start waving. He waves at me. I stumble over rocks and through brush. He sits on a blanket. Beneath his tall hat, sunglasses hide his eyes. When I get up close he removes his shades.

It's Big Al.

"Are we alive?" I ask.

He wrinkles up his long face, scrunches his nose and says, "Unfortunately, yes. They haven't let us out of school yet."

He looks me over good and careful.

"*I* look alive?" I ask again.

"Yes, you're alive. Want me to pinch you?"

His pinch doesn't prove a thing. My arm is numb.

I tell him what happened and he nods a wide holy smile. He sits me down by his side. Big Al doesn't talk. His face is a mask of sorrow and his eyes swim in pain. I think he's a sad man.

I look at Big Al from behind. His shoulders point
forward in a vee, like those of a beaten man. And his chin
is narrow and dimpled slightly inward.

"Why'd you come?" he asks me as he rocks back and
forth.

It's a good day to ask and a good day to tell.

"I don't know," I answer.

Big Al takes my neck in his hands and tells me to shut
my eyes.

I shut my eyes, clamp them tight and furrow my brow.
The more I squeeze, the more my head aches.

"Not everyone survives a bolt of lightning," he says.
"My people say that only medicine men get marked by a
strike."

"I don't feel like a medicine man," I say.

I don't feel like me and my memory seems gone.

I sit there looking up at the streaks of color cast by
the late-day sun. I feel the rocks under me. Columns of
ants pick through the weeds. The earth looks like marble.

"So, why are you traveling?" Big Al asks.

My breathing feels slow.

"Why are you traveling?" he asks again.

"Just trying to get to Oregon."

"But why are you traveling?" he asks one more time.

I feel lost in a sea of thoughts that float through my
head. The sky looks bent, like it's trying to fold across the
earth and envelop it whole.

"Why do you travel?" Big Al is asking me once again,
startling me out of my thoughts.

"I don't know," I shrug. "Why did the sky come down
on my head and shoot me up with a million volts? Why do
my feet refuse to stay still?

"I used to think I was looking for love. Now I'm just

looking for a warm touch and a soft, kind hand. Even a long, wet kiss would do. Maybe soon the earth will grab my feet and give me a piece of solid ground to find my soul. But for now I'll just keep moving along.

"Why do *you* travel, Big Al?"

I turn around and Big Al is gone. I wonder if he was ever there.

I turn again and the desert floor burns like a fire under the setting sun. Long streamers of cloud hang far away. And I see a pink colored highway glimmer on a hill.

I stare at the highway below, sparkling with pink granite, yellow broken lines and long, moving shadows, its steep turns rising to the sky. And I see that Big Al has left tracks in the sand.

He left a big smily face traced in the dirt, with words inscribed inside. They say, *"Melt down the mind, Daddy, go eat the road."*

22

The Quarter Pounder by the Bay

Somewhere down around 3,300 feet above sea level, I stop seeing pink neon highways. The doctor in Gallup says there might be some neurological damage and suggests a CAT scan. He says I suffer from physical exhaustion.

But I hear "cat scram" and scram I do for the nearest road I can step on.

I make a stop at a market to buy myself a lemonade Snapple. I suck it down in two easy swallows and decide to stick out my thumb. I am sick and tired of the dirty dog.

I make it all the way to Flagstaff in one easy ride. It's a van full of Deadheads who call me "old man." I bet myself fifty dollars that they're going to give me lice, and they do.

In Flagstaff I wander through town and settle by the road. I'm looking like a tramp with my single bag, and I wonder how I smell. I get a truck heaving trailers down the melting road to pull to a stop. The trucker is a good-looking weasel of a man, about forty-five, and tall.

He says hop in and I do.

He's got a box full of Taco Bell bean-and-cheese burritos. I know we'll get along. Just give him a knife hidden somewhere and he'll fit right in with all the psychos I've already met on the road.

His name is Bernie. He's from Tennessee. He's towing a truckload of conduits and keeps his cab real cold. I see his bunk in the back, all set up like a temple with a gold-framed picture set in a shrine. It's his wife and two kids.

"Going to Oakland!" he says, and I'm set for the ride.

I close my eyes and drift for a while. But not for long. He's a talker and wants me to be all ears for the next twenty hours.

Bernie. Hairy man. Big shoulders. About 190 pounds. He sits, shirt open, fuzzy belly and small gut hanging over the belt. I see his zipper's down.

Oh boy, I'm thinking. I bet he's got this one all planned. How many times a day does he pull over for a fair-looking ride and expect some oral repayment?

But he's a gump. A big old peanut-butter slob. His cap has a Denver Bronco logo on the visor. He's got a big old jar of Smucker's peanut butter sitting between his legs. Smells strong in here. Like a blend of four-day-old sweat and that truck-stop food stink.

He licks a spoon and offers me a taste from the jar.

"No thanks, I don't take bites off another man's spoon," I laugh. "But you know how to get rid of lice? I've got a bad case from my last ride."

"Yes," he nods. He points to a little bag in the back and says his lice killer ought to do.

We stop at the next truck stop, in Kingman, where I take a shower. He points the way for me. I walk into a long room with a wall full of lockers in it. I can smell the truckers.

I stand in the shower, scrubbing down with lice soap, getting them good under my arms. I pull a few off me and whip them to the floor. Then I hear old Bernie calling my name.

"Ayup, I'm in here, Bernie, just killing off these lice."

Bernie has no shame. He walks right on in and stands there looking at naked, soaking-wet me.

"Damn, don't you have a wife?" I say.

But that's not why he's here. He's bringing me a clean set of lice-free clothes. It's a T-shirt and new khaki pants.

"May not fit, but I thought you wouldn't want to be putting on the same old clothes when you hop out of the shower."

He leaves and gives me one last quick glance before he's gone.

Outside, in the truck, he's raring to go. He's all gassed up, zipped up and peanut-butter bloated.

I get in the truck, fresh and clean.

"Got family?" he asks when we hit the freeway.

"Of course I got family, we all got family. How you think we got here?" I say. I hate this question because I know what it means. It's a two-second judgment call to see if I'm a queer.

"I mean, you got a wife and kids?"

"I got five wives and twelve kids," I lie.

"Oh, you must be Mormon."

"Yeah, that's it." I roll my eyes.

For the next five hundred miles I have to listen to his sermon about the Lord. I knew the Lord had something to do with this ride, and I'm still not sure if it's a long-winded approach to just get me in his pants. One never knows.

When he really gets out of hand, I start quoting scripture. If there's one good thing my sixteen years of Bible study did, it gave me good practice for quoting verse. I hold my own. We are quoting verse all the way down the road. I finally tell him I'm gay. This sets the roof on fire.

When we finally pull over in Fresno, he's about to kick me out on the road. But I say, "Come on, Bernie, be a good sport. We have a right to our differences, don't we?"

I crash in the front while he sleeps for four hours in his clothes. He's wrapped in a mess of blankets and his little curtain is closed so tight a spider couldn't get through.

By the time we pull into Oakland the next day, he's driving me up the wall with last-ditch efforts to save my soul. I love the man for what a persistent salesman he is. But when I finally hop out the cab at the edge of Oakland, I soundly decline his offer to come back to the fold.

I leave him saying, "I'd rather go to hell a homosexual than live this life a lie."

The next morning I'm back in The City. Cold fog hits my head and my friend Viktor is no longer around. He's picked up and left for Oregon, I am told.

I give a call to the drive-away place for a northbound car and find a vehicle that needs to leave tomorrow. I hunch my shoulders and look around for a warm place. Almost June and it's cold as the Arctic.

I stand on the corner of Fourth and Brannan, buses cruising by. Every few minutes I become mesmerized by the funny electric sound, like so many gnats in my ear.

The Stockton 30 pulls up near the train station and I step on board. I clutch my quarters so tight my knuckles are blood-red. It seems as though several transients have settled in for a long sleep. They look as if they spend the day traveling the loop, seeing the city over and over in a dizzying circle, until the driver asks them to leave.

I drop my four quarters in the slot and head toward

the back of the extra-long bus pausing at the flexible midsection, where there are warnings not to touch the wall. I understand the warning and decide against sitting here because I know I will, of course, have to touch the wall just because the signs says not to.

In the back are the back-of-the-bus types. A man in a Forty-Niners hat is muttering to himself. Some kids in stocking caps are throwing lit matches at the floor. A heavyish man and woman wearing matching denim crowd a seat. I sit behind them because I like the smell of her hair—strawberry shampoo and maybe a twist of vanilla. Her deodorant smells like raspberries and rain.

I feel like following them for the day.

The bus lunges forward and we hold on for the ride. At the following stops the bus begins to fill with Asian women. Their fingers all look very agile and I can imagine them all sitting at sewing machines. Their chatter doubles in volume with every block. By the time we reach Folsom Street it sounds like a jungle, filled with birds. I expect to see Tarzan.

And a minute later he boards the bus. He has bleached hair and an admirable backside. His jeans are strategically ripped so you can see his ass when he bends a certain way. He is chewing gum louder than the Asian women's voices. But then the denim couple in front of me start talking.

"So what are you going to get?" she asks in a demanding sort of way.

"The Quarter Pounder," he replies.

"That's what you ordered last time."

"No I didn't. I had the cheeseburger with fries."

"I'm going to get the cheeseburger this time, but I want the large fries."

"We got enough money?"

"Well, then I'll forget the fries. I'll have some of yours."

"I'm not getting fries."

"You're always getting fries."

I am absorbed in their discussion. I am hungrily dreaming of sitting with them at their table, wherever they are headed, and ordering the same. I decide I would share my fries with her even if she doesn't ask.

"Maybe I'll just order a chocolate shake and forget the cheeseburger," she says.

"Why? You think you can have some of *my* burger?"

"No, I just feel like a shake instead."

"Good, then I won't have to share my Quarter Pounder."

Their talk is making me hungry. They go on and on about the order, which they've obviously done countless times before. I sort of admire them for still finding ways to discuss variations on the same old theme. I feel so identified with their obsession that I dream of a serene life, filled with just this one decision. Every day could be a choice. To order the Quarter Pounder or not to order the Quarter Pounder. All of life could be regulated by it. And I would be at peace.

I am so fascinated that I don't care that the bus has filled to capacity by the time we hit Market Street. So many small Asian women are aboard that I want to be like them. I want to chatter in that clucky sound and not seem racist. I can feel my honorable Chinese motherhood rising to the surface. My feet feel small and my fingers feel like threading a bobbin. I can smell ginger and I begin to wonder if I am on drugs.

Suddenly I notice my potential dinner mates are

exiting. I rush for the door in a panic that it won't open and I will have to yell "Back door" in a loud voice with everyone watching, knowing I'm a loser. But the door opens and I follow them off the bus.

We walk toward a Burger King, with me several steps back. I imagine us all walking arm-in-arm like old friends, discussing the finer merits of our soon-to-be-purchased Quarter Pounders. Our pace quickens as we near the entrance.

We file in, walking up to the smiling clerk at the counter and the man proudly says, "Gimme a Quarter Pounder, please!"

The smell of grease is strong. Then I notice that Burger King is home of the Whopper, not the Quarter Pounder. Are my friends unaware of the difference? The man behind the counter tries to correct them. "You mean the Whopper?" he asks. But it goes over their heads.

The denim woman orders a Quarter Pounder with large fries and coffee. Then she looks at me quizzically. Maybe she recognizes me from the bus.

I order the same as them and sit two booths away, basking in the feeling that we are family. She wolfs her burger, but she does it with her pinkies held out. I can see she is well brought up. The room feels like home, with my denim couple at my side.

A wall of glass barely separates us from Market Street. A man standing outside hungrily watches all of us eat. I can feel the urgency in his eyes. We make a connection, but I am not sure over what. He enters the Burger King and passes by me. He walks up to my denim friends and lunges for their remaining food. He comes up with a handful of fries and the coveted pickle, stuffing it into his mouth.

She looks nonplussed, as if this happens every day. She calmly clutches her coffee as if retrieving a drink from an errant child before it gets spilled. She shoos him away with her pinkie and wipes crumbs from the corner of her lips.

But then management gets involved and the whole thing turns ugly. It's like having the police burst in while you're carving the Thanksgiving turkey.

"What's with the Gestapo routine? He just grabbed my food, for Christ's sake," she's saying to the manager. She lets out a slight burp but the offender is dragged away, kicking and screaming, leaving an aroma of the unwashed behind him.

The manager offers the denim couple another Whopper, free, which they accept, but ask for it to go.

I follow them out to the street and across the plaza toward Polk. In the Tenderloin shadows begin to lengthen. Dusk is falling and the streetlights cast an interesting warmth in the cool foggy air. I can feel the fog rolling in and wonder why I didn't think to bring a coat. I split off to begin looking for a home for the night, and bid farewell to my Quarter Pounder pals.

23

Return to the Sea

I've had a sick feeling in my stomach all morning. A psychic sort of thing. Like my life's never going to be the same.

I walk to the drive-away place and pick up another car. It's a 1973 Thunderbird in mint condition with a big blue gear shift, ladylike, on a dash of fuzzy gold nap carpet, and a hefty medallion is hanging from the mirror.

Looks like a drug-smuggling car if ever there was one. I head across the Golden Gate, racing from out of the city. I'm going the long way up the coast to Portland.

I cruise through Marin City, turn off at Mt. Tam and head over to the blue Pacific. Down the mountain the ocean flares jewel-like with the sun streaming across the waves. Surfers ride the frothy curls. I pass Stinson Beach and sense the salt settling in my pores.

I feel freedom biting like a hungry calf at the belly of my soul. I toss words out the window and make an oath of my love for the sea. Nothing but God between me and the ocean below.

Bodega Bay flees like a bullet out my rearview mirror. Rolling spring-green hills covered with sagebrush bloom under the sky. I curse the day anyone tries to take this away from me. The road's my lover and latent whore, slapping, bruising, crying against my rubber tires. I hug the coast and finally pull off at Russian Gulch in a little dale that meanders to the sea.

There's dust in the air but only a few cars in the dirt lot. It's my day at the beach and time to wash some road dirt out from under my nails.

Through a jungle of leaves and gnarled trees I follow a creek that ends at the edge of a freshwater pool. The ocean beats on the sand a hundred yards away. Naked, I dive head-first into a sharp, wet cold that shrinks my balls and freezes my head.

I yip and yell, running about like an elk. My eyes open clear and wide. The sun glints off my skin. I walk across the beach, clutching my clothes at my waist. A few rubber-booted fishermen cast their lines out into the surf, then push their poles deep into the sand. Their wool caps and giant yellow coats protect them against the wind.

They think I'm nuts.

I follow a path over blue rocks that wrap around a cliff. The surf crashes at my heels, spraying pearly white foam over my head. It feels like the North Pole even in the middle of spring.

There's another beach around the rocks. It's all mine, the stretch of sand like a deserted island. I run like a madman across the beach and back, licking the salt from the back of my hand. The ocean swallows me up and bites my feet, cradles my body in her power. I surf the waves for hours, like a fish returned to home. One giant wave finally picks me up and knocks me hard against the shore.

And here I lie.

My thoughts float in half a day of sleep on the sand. I

think of Morocco and desert rides, caves of memory, faraway places, faces from long ago.

Hours drift by.

I hear a yelp. A tiny voice from another world.

Flies buzz around my nose.

I hear another yelp, a little louder, and open my eyes. The sun is past midday and the surf is rising. The tide is rushing in, nibbling at my toes.

I hear another yelp.

My eyes strain in the sunlight. I look up. I feel bright, pink and red. I'm sunburned and lying there nude. I look for my clothes. But they're gone, washed out to sea. I'd left them three feet down and the waves have long since eaten them whole.

"Help!" Someone yells.

This time I stand up. I hear a voice coming from the water. I see two hands and a head bobbing up and down in the ocean, waving side to side. It's a red-haired girl struggling in the surf. A wave picks her up and throws her down near large jagged rocks at the end of the beach. She grabs at the rocks but the undertow pulls her out. She goes under, long and deep, then bobs up, yelling for help again and again.

I don't know what to do.

I wade out into the surf. The undertow is strong. My feet go down.

"Swim parallel," I yell. "Don't fight the waves."

I yell again for her to swim. She starts struggling across the waves, following my lead.

It begins to work. She swims away from the rocks, along the beach, twenty yards from shore.

I wade in, up to my waist, coaching her along.

"Now dive for the beach," I yell when a wave begins to curl over her.

She dives in and the wave pushes her to me. Two waves more and I stretch out my octopus arms. I tug and pull with all my might. She holds me tight, shaking, crying, clutching at my bony arms. She's a bundle of nerves beached on the sand.

I drag her ashore, pull her farther up the beach and bury her under warm sand. We sit quietly in the sun.

"Who are you?" she finally asks, her teeth chattering. "You saved my life."

I beg to differ. "If I weren't such a coward, I would have jumped in. All I did was coax you along."

"No, you saved my life," she says. "I'm Sandra, and I owe you."

We spend a while debating the point. Half buried, her body is warming up. Her face thaws from blue to pink.

"Where are your clothes?" she finally asks, nodding toward my shriveled penis, shrunken by the icy surf.

"They washed out with the waves," I say with a smile, cupping my private parts.

"Guess we have to wait for the tide to go out," she says, pointing at the waves covering the rocks.

It finally dawns on me that I'm stuck. Then I spot some long strings of seaweed, which I use to wrap and cover my bare body.

Sandra is a strong-looking girl, wearing Spandex shorts and a bright yellow top.

"Where you from?" I ask.

"Santa Rosa. I work in a lab. Nothing glamorous. Went to school in Cotati. Where are you from?"

"All over. I've traveled Mexico, Canada, Spain,

Belgium, you know, the European thing, and uh, Morocco..."

Sandra sits up in the wind. "I had a friend who spent some time in Morocco. He had tales to tell."

"Yeah, it was wild for me, too," I answer.

"My friend traveled through the desert on the back of a truck full of dead goats!" she says.

"That's wild , I...What did you say?"

"I said my friend traveled through the desert."

"But the goats?" I sit up, tugging the seaweed around my shoulders.

"Oh yeah, he rode on a truck full of dead goats."

I flip a rock across the sand and stop talking for a second, looking out at the sun as it dips into the sea.

"What was your friend's name?" My foot taps on the sand.

"I love the sunset," she says.

"What was your friend's name?" I repeat a little too harshly.

"Oh...Joseph."

"Joseph!" I scream, jerking up. "Did you say Joseph?"

"Yeah, Joseph. He was Swedish."

I sit stiff. My ears point toward her. "Was he tall and blond?"

"Yes, why?"

"Was he traveling with a friend?"

"Yes." Sandra looks startled.

I'm up on my feet tall and tense, my eyes unblinking. She also stands.

I grab her arms. "Do you know who he traveled with?"

"Not really." She pulls away.

"Was he called Peter?"

"Peter—right. His name *was* Peter."

I grab her harder, so tight her hands are turning blue. "Peter…are you serious? You know Joseph and Peter?"

"What's wrong?" She shoves away my arms.

"I can't believe it. You know Joseph and Peter—I'm going to explode! How?"

"Joseph was in Cotati to see his girlfriend, Patricia."

"His girlfriend?"

"She's my best friend since grade school. She met Joseph in Europe in seventy-two and they came back together. We lived together for six months."

"Oh, my God. I wonder if it's the same Joseph. Tell me about the truck ride," I say.

"He said he traveled through Morocco with Peter and an American. They rode trucks through the Sahara on top of…"

"Dead goats!" we both say.

"How do you know all of this?" she asks.

"I'm the American!"

"You are?" she screams. "That's wild!"

"Yeah!" I stand grinning and shaking my head back and forth, twisting my heels deep in the sand.

"What a coincidence." She smiles.

"This is more than a coincidence. It's the biggest miracle I've ever heard of. I can't believe you know them. Are you in touch?"

"Yes."

I come rushing at her again. This time she's not so scared. "You know how to reach them?"

"Yes. They're in Sweden."

"And Peter, you've met him?"

"For a day, once. He came over four years ago with Patricia and Joseph. He was down in the city."

"You saw him?" I feel like a madman on the edge of time. My internal clock turns brutally backward more than twenty years. I hold my head in my hands. I stand for a long moment, the question held on my lips. I am afraid of what I'll hear.

We sit down on the sand.

"What was he like?"

"Peter? He was quiet and withdrawn but very handsome, with clear blue eyes."

"And blond hair, bright as the sun," I add.

"Well, not really. He was bald!"

"Bald?" Somehow I couldn't imagine this. "Well, wasn't he the sexiest man you'd ever seen?"

"Well, he was sort of pudgy."

"Pudgy? Are you sure it was Peter?"

"Yes."

"But he had golden skin!"

"Um, sort of pasty and wrinkled."

"It really was Peter?" I ask again.

"Yes, it was Peter."

"Oh, I see. So it was the three of them."

"No, there were four."

"Who was the fourth?"

"Peter's wife."

"Oh, I see." My voice lowers.

"Are you okay?" she asks.

"Yeah." I look out to the sea and remember the desert and the border with the camels and guns. I carefully recreate the details of our parting, abrupt as it was.

And I remember the look in his eyes.

I guess we all have our first true love. I guess we all have that magical person forever etched in our mind, the place where dreams and reality converge, allowing a lover to walk through our door.

Peter was that lover for me. He was a hand that held my sorrow and hugged me in my sleep. He faced death with me when we believed we were bidding the world goodbye. And he was the person through whom I discovered my passion for men. The memory of him was inseparable from that last look on his face.

And finally I face the truth. The Peter of my dreams and the Peter of real life are two different beings. I am sad that they must at long last become one in my mind.

We sit, Sandra and I, holding each other, shivering in the cooling night. I cry in her arms and she doesn't ask why. And I feel so old.

Less than an hour goes by before we see a flashlight coming down a trail on the cliff at the far end of the beach. We sprint across the sand and come upon two men fishing.

We race up the trail and in half an hour are back at our cars. I scramble for clothes and leave behind my seaweed.

Sandra gives me a hug and a slip of paper with Joseph's address in Sweden. She assures me he will know how to reach Peter.

We wave goodbye and I turn up Route One.

I take the highway with force and speed around curves. The moon casts bright, long shadows across the boundary of hills. I hold the fluttering slip of paper at my window. I hold it across the edge of time. With a kiss I let it fly from my fingers and out to the sea.

24

Last Thumb, My Engine Hums

"Stay on the road, damn it," I yell myself awake.

It's next day, noon, and I'm crossing into Oregon, nearly asleep at the wheel. My right tire has drifted into the ditch by the road, almost hitting the metal mile marker signs that go whizzing by.

I come to a stop just in time. Ahead, tangled cartons of plastic are strewn open, littering the road. A tractor-trailer truck with its doors thrown open has scraped long jagged gouges in the asphalt and sits amid a horrible mess.

"Accident ahead." A white-collared, Christian-looking man stands, hands outstretched, ball-point pen clipped to his pocket and officialdom stamped on his brow. But he's just doing his good deed for the day.

"No shit," I say.

But the real event is farther up ahead.

A woman is having a baby in the oncoming lane. She stopped her car right in the middle of the road and swung open her doors, with her feet dangling out. She's making squealing sounds.

"Water broke," someone yells like it's the ten o'clock news.

"You can see the head. Look!" another yells.

About twenty cars are all stacked up on both sides behind the truck going north and behind her going south. There's no room to pass.

"Why didn't she just pull off the side of the road?" I dare to ask.

"Guess she felt the head poking out and just stopped then and there," chuckled the driver of the blown-out rig.

A big electric wire crosses the road overhead and half a dozen squirrels are playing tightrope on it. Flocks of noisy bluejays squawk disapproval of our roadside invasion.

A few women are leaning their heads into the car. One of them is wearing white cowboy boots, a plaid shirt and sunglasses pushed back on her forehead. She barks orders and knows what to do when it comes to giving birth. She's got a crucifix the size of a road sign around her neck and there are nine kids in her station wagon.

"Push, push!" I can hear her yell.

"Yeah, yeah, yeah!" Two longhair grunge kids are mocking the scene.

I can't see the woman but can hear her scream. She must be twisting in her seat and twitching her legs. Her car rocks on the road. The woman moans. Others stand by protectively, not allowing us men to lend a hand.

The highway's jammed as more cars stack up. The trucker has radioed for help and he sits in his cab smoking a cigar.

Suddenly there's a gagging sound. A few of the women are smiling. Faces are straining to look into the car. Half a second later we all hear the burst of a gurgling voice that sounds like a kitty cat's whine, and then a loud shout.

"It's a girl, it's a girl!" they're yelling.

Everybody's carrying on, clapping like it's our own little road baby. The big woman comes out of the car, her hands red. She pulls at her breasts like two loaves of peasant bread.

The mother is sitting up and looking out of breath. She holds the little thing in a white silky scarf that turns a splotchy red.

The women shoo the men away.

We try to get a better look but they block our view like we're perverts for wanting to see the baby. They're all so uptight. This adds to my list of sound reasons why Oregon conservatives bother me so.

The two long-legged teenagers in the car behind are snapping on gum and playing their radio loud. They start rocking their car back and forth yelling, "Big fucking deal, another mouth to feed."

The sun beats down on sweating brows and keys begin to jangle. The birth car gets rolled off to the side of the road.

We men get our ten-second glance when we drive by.

I turn my sunburnt face toward the road and crank up the stereo monstrously loud. I frizz out my chest hairs and spin the medallion hanging off the rearview mirror.

The long roaring sound of my high-powered engine pulls me down the highway toward Grants Pass. The hot spring sun puts me in a hundred-dollar mood. I feel like a rich man going home.

About ten miles from Gold Beach, I'm going kind of wild around a curve. Double-dot reflectors are going bumpity bump and a twisted line of trees leans over the ditch.

I see a thumb.

This thumb pokes out of a fingerless black glove. With a long pair of skintight black tights, the hitchhiker is the very image of a con man in flight. He chews on a candy bar and pours a sixty-cent Coke down his throat from his left hand. His hair stands tall like an afro in the wind.

I breeze past, ignoring him at first. He flips me the bird, then turns around and moons me, white cheeks and all. I'm watching from the rearview mirror and this gets me to stop because I like what I see.

If he's advertising it, I'm game.

I idle by a white-fenced farm with a small herd of billy goats blabbing at the gate. They stand on their back legs looking at me like I'm going to set them free.

Finally up strolls my hitchhiker. He lugs a heavy-looking green-and-orange duffel bag full of clothes and a little string bag full of food. He tosses a candy wrapper to the side of the road and wipes his face on his sleeve. He strolls as if he's got all the time in the world.

"Get the hell in," I yell as he drags on like a Disney flick at slow speed. "I'm in a hurry."

"So where are you going?" he asks before he's in.

"Portland," I yell.

With his burly black beard, he's a dead ringer for Charles Manson, though considerably younger. He's a short grungemeister with ripped-up clothes, wrinkled seams, a plaid shirt, a pink mouth and thick eyebrows. But his baby-fresh breath smells like mint, or maybe Bazooka gum.

"Name's Atlas," he says.

"Atlas? I'm sure. Who gave you that name?"

"My uncle. His name was Boots."

"I don't believe you," I say.

Atlas is a road babe. Only twenty-two and from Brazil, he's a small man with warm eyes and a lisp that carries like the wind. He's carting too much shit in his bag and I tell him so.

"Got to lighten up if you're going to do the road thing. What are you carrying?"

"Records," he says.

He opens up his duffel and lets me flip through his albums. Must be twenty pounds of vinyl in there.

"What the hell are you carrying around all that for?"

"I collect," he says.

"You brought them from Brazil?"

"Yeah. I may never go back."

"You're nuts."

We both laugh. He has a funny laugh, half a giggle, but mostly a tease with enough madness thrown in to rattle my cage. He rocks in his seat like he's riding a boat. I smell stink coming up from his shoes and tell him he needs a bath.

"So give me a bath."

"I don't have a washcloth or water," I say.

"Just use your hands and my Coke," he replies.

I study him a second before taking off. His eyes are wide like a deer's. His lashes blink against the steady warm air and I swear he's winking.

"Are you flirting with me?" I ask.

"Maybe," he says.

We ride silently and I like it that way. I look at the road up ahead. Patches of sun bright as Wonder Bread slice through the tall forest.

I keep my mouth shut and don't ask him a thing. I want no story, no life history, no sad tale. I just want his company, nice and quiet, for the ride ahead.

Our silence continues for miles. But soon, as we come into a town, he's acting all hot and sweaty.

"Atlas...that's really your name?" I ask again.

"Yes," he says in his Brazilian accent.

Young Atlas smells like a skunk, but he is a grungy hunk. He wears a shirt that isn't long enough and his hairy back pokes out the bottom. He scrapes dirt out from his fingernails and ties his hair in little knots. Bubble gum pops out the side of his mouth.

I pull over for gas in Agness and plan to leave him there on the side of the road, his smell is so bad.

But it doesn't work. Taking my hints, he jumps out, rips off several lengths of paper towels, leans over the station's radiator water hose and starts hosing himself down. He pulls off his stretch pants and shirt. Hairy as an ape, he stands in his striped jockey underwear with its bulging basket while he takes an impromptu shower next to the pumps.

This guy is gnarly. But I like his funky style.

The attendant comes unglued. "What the hell are you doing? Put your clothes back on."

Parents are covering little eyes. Big adult eyes glare heavy with judgment at the nearly naked young Brazilian taking his shower.

I pay for the gas.

Atlas pats himself dry, tosses his clothes in the backseat and says he's ready to go.

"Well, that's an improvement, I must say so."

Atlas smiles wide.

"So where are you going?" I finally ask.

He's going to Ashland for an off-the-books restaurant job and wants to look fresh. Water drips out of his flattened hair as he pulls dirt balls the size of eggs out of his shoes. His socks lie across the dash to dry.

We chirp down the road singing a song. Atlas is chewing on a coffee bean and scraping his knees up under the dash, picking at puckered mosquito bites on the edge of his legs. My eyes follow his woolly mammoth body hair up his thighs. I watch him rocking in his seat and mother lust enters my mind.

Long road, no sex, not good, I think to myself.

He pulls out a pocket knife and is clipping his toes. I swear that if I see one more knife in a young man's hands on this trip, I am going to bury them all—the knives that is.

"Knives or guns, knives or guns, everybody's traveling with knives or guns," I yell my disapproval.

Atlas looks confused and puts away his knife. He sits back in his seat, sniffing the air. "Smells like Coppertone," he says.

I point to my big bottle of suntan protection, and point at my shiny head.

"Can't be too careful," I say.

I open the cap with one hand and am going to rub some more on when he grabs it from me and squirts a big old glob on top my head.

"Why'd you do that?" I yell.

I look like a vanilla sundae. I wipe off the glob and in friendly revenge smear it on his face. He wipes it off his face and smears it on my chest. I wipe it off my chest and smear it on his thighs. He wipes it off his thighs and smears it on my lap. I smear it on his groin.

"You're crazy," I yell. "Who the hell are you?"

"Maybe I'm your boyfriend," he laughs, his eyes sparkling.

He is wickedly teasing me, playing with my head. He pulls out a book of matches, lights them off the striker and throws them lit in the backseat.

"That's enough! You're out of control." I pull over and tell him to get out, my finger pointed hard to the side of the door.

"Oh, do I have to?" he baby-doll pleads, mocking me.

I nod my head and he's about to get out when he wipes off his smile and says with head bowed like a choirboy in need of confession, "I'll behave. I'll do whatever you want. Whatever..." and he puts his hand on my leg.

"Do you think I'm gay?" I finally say.

"Well, aren't you?"

"What if I weren't?"

"Well, there's always a first time." He smiles.

"Oh my!" I feel through the glove box and pull out a cheap cigar. I light it from the matches and blow a smoke ring over the cheap fuzzy dash.

"You are a scene. Are you this loose with everyone?" He nods.

I toss back my head and feel my tired hot feet and socks full of sand. He sulks in the corner, his head out the window, wondering what I will do.

I finally smile, get out of the car and walk toward the woods, expecting he'll follow. He trails me with his wild eyes, then jumps out and tags along. I get far from the road and settle next to a tree. I put out my cigar and watch him coming up the trail.

"Oregon has laws about this. It's a very Christian place," I say.

Atlas smiles a broad, seductive smile. He walks toward me, then leaps down on his knees, squawking like a duck and rubbing his belly. He's a prankster, he is.

"I don't give a shit about your laws," he laughs.

I believe him.

My thumb presses into the fold of his arm and my fingers follow the bones on his side. My boot rocks like a baby at the base of his groin. I feel the lonely taste of a long bottled-up journey. Desire creases across my head.

His hair curves off his face and his lips pout up in a kiss. He leans forward as if in prayer and rolls his face across my jeans.

Then he wrestles me down and bites me till I scream. And I finally get the kiss that I was so long looking for.

25

Welcome Home

Hours later, we bring half the forest and a swarm of bugs back to the car. He's changed into rosy red pants and a long summer shirt with a silk-screened cactus on it. We share a cigar and crank the music loud.

I feel like such a sleaze.

We move down the highway like we're watching a drive-in movie from the front of the car. We seem to move in slow motion under the purple skies and over the yellow curves of the Oregon road.

Pushing east, away from the coast, we drive the Thunderbird among the wooded hills. Atlas flips through country channels and finds k.d. lang. Tall plumes of smoke billow off the rolling fields. It looks like fire on the open range.

I pull off in Grants Pass to gas up and let my rider go on his way. Atlas packs across the tarmac, bidding me a sassy goodbye.

The attendant does the work while I sit at the pump. I stare at the clicking dollars on the meter when, my God, who do I see but those two stinking cowboys who I met here a month before. They pull up alongside in their old rusted-

out Honda Civic in all their cowboy, firecracking glory.
They're wearing the same damn hats they wore then.

I feel so cocky full of myself that no rubberneck
rednecks could come close to fazing me now. Plus, I've got
a bigger car.

These two losers are out fumbling around under
their hood, drunk off their asses. Just when I'm finished,
one of them looks at me.

I see a slow look of recognition creeping into his
Neanderthal brain. By the time he's got me figured out, I
speed away, blowing him a juicy wet kiss goodbye.

I can see their faces redder than hell.

I pull over to a phone booth, its windows broken and
marked up, the Yellow Pages torn and scattered across the
floor. I call in for two weeks' worth of voice mail messages,
thirteen in all.

Five from Jim wondering where the hell I am, another
six from bill collectors who won't ever leave me alone. One
from Viktor Fidele, who moved to eastern Oregon and isn't
feeling very well, and the last from Samantha down in
Memphis. She says she and Chris say hello.

Then I party on down the highway, settling into high
speed. It's just me and my Thunderbird cruising the road,
scooting across Oregon with the new grass filling the hills.

I see cop cars chasing a fugitive and a fire truck
chasing a fire.

Thunderclaps and the rain starts to pour. I hydro-
plane it north and join a parade of souped-up Pontiacs
entering Puddle Town. I exit downtown, park and join the
mob of shoppers on the sidewalks. I walk into the world's
biggest bookstore, through a maze of print covering a city
block, and I look for a phone. I give my friend Jim "the
Mad Monk" a call to let him know I'm in Portland.

I drive madly across town with visions of burritos dancing in my head. I hit the nearest Taco Bell and order three dozen bean-and-cheese burritos for a welcome-back meal.

About three o'clock, I pull into Southwest. I feel like a pigeon returning to roost. I deliver my drive-away car to a big old lady in a pink suit and frilly bow tie.

I make my way over to Dot's Cafe on the grunge side of Portland. The fresh rain has left wet reflections and the sunset makes a brilliant pink glow, flashing light across the road.

Jim comes driving down the street in that big old painted motor home of ours. The colors are streaming, paint is peeling, and it looks like the damn circus is in town.

Jim pulls her up to the curb and bounds out with a big open smile. His arms spread wide around me and his big belly folds across my ribs.

He pulls me on board.

My cat, Dolly, sits on the dash and the good old funky smells of motor-home life come flooding into my nose and settle on my tongue.

"Welcome home, Mike!" Jim says, jumping up and down. "How was your trip? You ready to roll?"

I look at him with a five-mile smile and turn my eyes upward. I hold my thoughts close to my heart and bow my head to the floor. I inhale a big burning breath of my motor-home air. With bloodshot eyes, a mouth full of burritos, ten thousand miles under my belt and a shake of my head, I say nice and clear, long and slow, "Jim...you'll never believe what I've been through. And yes, I'm ready to roll!"

ACKNOWLEDGMENTS

A hearty thanks to a million miles of friends who have supported this solo adventure of mine.

And with greatest thanks to Jim Crotty, Doug Brantley, Mom and Jay, Jane Dystel, Bruce Shostak and Aaron Lauer.

The first version of this book was stolen in its entirety in San Francisco.

The subsequent and final version of this book was written at the Matador Motel in Chico, California, Room 31, under heavy guard.

May the first version rest in peace.